What People Are Saying About

Joan and Roger Alive in the Afterlife

A compelling read. The fascinating story of Spillane's search to prove the existence of life beyond life provides intriguing evidence and poses even more questions about the biggest question of all.
Ian Williams, senior English teacher, and subject of *Uncanny: BBC TV, Series 1, Episode 2, The Bearpark Poltergeist*

For those of us who want reassurance that the afterlife exists then this book is a must read. Jeremy Spillane and wife, Caroline, are guided by her deceased parents, Roger and Joan, on a metaphysical adventure the likes of which will go down in paranormal research history. The use of the SLS camera, along with other corroborative tools and talented psychic mediums, allow Roger and Joan to present themselves in a clear and dramatic fashion providing proof of the afterlife. As a paranormal researcher with considerable experience using the SLS camera, I was impressed with the methods Jeremy and Caroline devised to better assure that false images did not occur. The link to the videos of their actual contacts and communications enhanced my enthusiasm for the accounts of Roger, Joan, Jeremy and Caroline and I am sure it will for you. Read this book and watch the videos – you will not be disappointed.
Mark Wentz M.A, retired particle and nuclear physicist

Wow, what a truly honest and varied account of paranormal, but to me, normal spirit activity! Sensitively put together by Jeremy with his natural and humble approach. Enlightening!
Stephen Holbrook, UK's Premier Psychic Medium

Having read through this remarkable story, I feel the journey has proven life after death is an interesting step. This book shows the love and contact by a lovely couple who are always with us, even when at times we do not believe. Well done and keep up the interaction!
Mark Penn, Stonebridge Associated Colleges, Diploma in Parapsychology, demonologist

Joan and Roger Alive in the Afterlife

Jeremy Spillane

Joan and Roger Alive in the Afterlife

More than two years later, Joan and Roger continue to appear every time I turn on the SLS camera, and they communicate with us

Jeremy Spillane

London, UK
Washington, DC, USA

First published by Sixth Books, 2026
Sixth Books is an imprint of Collective Ink Ltd.,
Unit 11, Shepperton House, 89 Shepperton Road, London, N1 3DF
office@collectiveinkbooks.com
www.collectiveinkbooks.com
www.6th-books.com

For distributor details and how to order please visit the 'Ordering' section on our website.

ISBN: 978 1 78535 625 4
978 1 917704 15 1 (ebook)
Library of Congress Control Number: 2025902949

A CIP catalogue record for this book is available from the British Library.

Design: Lapiz Digital Services

UK: Printed and bound by CPI Group (UK) Ltd, Croydon, CR0 4YY
Printed in North America by CPI GPS partners
Pls add the following GPSR disclaimer:

The manufacturer's authorised representative in the EU for product safety is:
eucomply OÜ - Pärnu mnt 139b-14, 11317 Tallinn, Estonia, hello@ eucompliancepartner.com, www.eucompliancepartner.com

Contents

Dedication

This book is dedicated to my wonderful, amazing wife, Caroline, without who's gentle but persistent prodding and help I would never have found her parents on camera, after their funerals.

This book is also dedicated to Joan and Roger, who have proved beyond doubt to me that they are part of my soul group, along with several other family members and friends. I look forward to our next earthly adventure together in our next physical lifetimes.

Within this soul group are my parents, Thelma and Frank, without you and the upbringing you gave me, I wouldn't have even dreamt of writing this book. Dad would turn his hand to anything – his inspiration has made me do the same, to question everything and to embark on a quest like no other.

I'd like to thank all the people who have helped us to relay Joan and Roger's story – you all know who you are. Without all of you, what Roger has learnt in the last two years wouldn't have seen the light of day. I'm so grateful to Roger for his persistence, and for engineering all the details to enable this book to be published. I really do hope, on Roger's behalf, that anyone who knew him reads his story – he really did want you to know what he is up to now; he's sure you'll be fascinated to hear what he has found out since his body expired.

I sincerely need to thank Sixth Books for having the faith in me necessary to offer me a contract. It was Caroline who discovered Sixth Books, a publisher I hadn't heard of. At that point, I just knew they were the publishers for Roger's book, so I aimed it fairly and squarely at them.

Finally, I'd like to thank you, the reader. You are the final and most important link in the chain. It's you who Roger is trying to reach with his amazing true story. With his teacher's hat on, Roger is wanting to tell you just what he has discovered very recently. What had seemed an impossibility to Roger while on this Earth, he now knows is genuinely real. From his spiritual vantage point, he is educating all of us – he just wants us to listen, and to view the evidence he's showing us.

His book doesn't follow the rules; it's not like any other book. This is why it is not being done in the conventional way. Roger's story is still evolving as he reveals more to us, almost weekly – keep up to date by reviewing the social media. The marketing and promotion aren't working in the conventional way either. This is why Roger is relying on you, the reader, to tell your friends and family, anyone who might be interested, to read his book. If it changes your outlook on this whole Life and Death conundrum, as it has mine, then Roger is eager for you to pass the message on.

Preface

I had never had any ambition to write a book. I was very well aware of just what a massive undertaking it was, and I had never been inspired by anything in particular that warranted writing a book. Over the years, I had written various, occasional magazine articles, in specialist magazines, letters in newspapers etc., but a book? I had never wanted to do that.

When my in-laws died, however, well, what they did, after they died, changed everything in my life. Suddenly, everything I thought I knew about life, was turned on its head. What Joan and Roger have revealed to their daughter Caroline, and me, has been breathtaking, almost unbelievable, truly awe-inspiring. Although Joan, I think, still believed in God and religion when she died, I am 99% certain Roger didn't – that's certainly what he always told me – "There is no life after death." The way he lived his life on Earth suggests that he really thought physical death was the end of everything. As soon as he died, he has been giving us messages, to tell us he was wrong – there actually really is an afterlife.

The purpose of this book is to share our stories with you, the reader, both mine and Caroline's, as well as Joan and Roger's. Everything in this book is true, exactly as it happened.

Roger was a book fanatic, and an educator, so he has definitely inspired and co-opted me into writing this book; indeed, co-opted me into *co-writing* this book. It is no marketing ploy to say that Roger is the co-author, he really has led the way, pulled all the strings – I've merely had to follow his lead. Everything I have done for this book has fallen into place, and one of the mediums featured in this book, Ali Mather, has confirmed that to be the case – that Roger and two other spirit guides of mine have been directing me in the planning and writing of this book.

Ali Mather told me that one of my spirit guides had changed a few months back, and the new one has taken the plan for the book in a slightly different direction, making it more reader-friendly – I *had* changed the plan a few months ago, and I am now certain this new plan is the right one. I hadn't realised that I was being guided to do this by someone other than Roger.

I am really over the moon that this book has made it into print, and I really am happy that whoever is behind it has made it happen in the way that it has.

Most chapters in the book have a video attached, which can be viewed by using your smartphone camera on the QR code on the front cover. This will take you to the YouTube channel where the videos for each chapter are available to watch.

Alternatively, you can search YouTube using the title of this book, *Joan and Roger Alive in the Afterlife.*

Finally, you can enter this link into your internet browser to do the same:

https://www.youtube.com/@joanandrogerafterlife/videos

Some of the videos are quite long, but I was unable to make them short, as they would have lost most of their incredible details – I wanted you, the reader, to be able to see exactly what we have seen, so you can be just as amazed as we are. If you don't want to watch such lengthy videos, the one for the first chapter is only 5 minutes long and gives a great taster of what Joan and Roger's story is about.

This book couldn't have happened without the help of several people, who I would now like to thank: Firstly, Caroline, my wife, has been totally instrumental in inspiring and pushing me to do this, gently, but persistently, nudging me to buy the equipment to find her parents' spirits on camera, and to communicate with them. I've had the most enjoyable and steep learning curve, in using the equipment and in learning about everything *paranormal*.

Next, Caroline's best friend, Jo, who lives in Australia, has very generously edited the book and inspired me to get it finished. As an English teacher and someone with great spiritual awareness, she is the perfect person to do this.

Ali Mather, a fantastic medium, and now a very good friend to Caroline and me, has motivated me to complete the book, and helped me visualise the final end result.

Another person to thank for their help is Trish Towell, who was training to be a qualified medium within the Spiritualist Church. She helped me to get some spiritual awareness, as she could sense I had various issues at the time and would benefit from spiritual insight. She very generously gave me many weekly sessions and set me on the path which eventually led me to believe in life after death – this all happened around the time of Joan's death.

There are several other people to thank, but they all need to remain anonymous. The lady who owns the memorial company which made Joan and Roger's headstone was so inspiring, a breath of fresh air, so generous with her time – we were even invited to see the headstones being made – what skill those craftspeople have!

Although you might initially think otherwise, especially if judging it by the cover, this book is not a sensationalist ghost hunting book in the style of many ghost hunting programmes. Roger would be aghast if that were the case. It is an educational book, showing you, the reader, what we have all learnt since Joan and Roger lost their physical bodies. There has been a lot of learning to be done, for us and for them. I'm so honoured that they have both taken the trouble to firstly get our attention, then secondly, to share their new-found knowledge with us. We want to share with you everything they have shown us.

The lower part of the front cover is a still, a screen shot, taken from the SLS camera footage, showing Joan's and Roger's spirits on camera for the very first time. These green stick figures are how the special camera indicates that there is a spirit there.

It's been hard sometimes keeping motivated to write this book, because many people didn't want to talk about what we were doing, what we were finding out about the afterlife. Many family members haven't been able to talk, but I'm hoping that when they can read Joan and Roger's story at their own pace, they will appreciate just what we have been so privileged to witness.

If you would like to ask me anything, if I can help you in any way, then please message me. All the contact details are at the end of Chapter 10.

Introduction

Roger was my father-in-law. He was adamant that there was no life after death. He died in April 2022. Since then, he has proved, on camera, that he lives on as a spirit, without his physical body.

This book is all about Roger and Joan and the incredible lengths they have gone to, to prove to all of humanity living on Earth that there is an afterlife.

Everything in this book is what Roger wants everyone to know. As far as I can find, it's also the first time in human history that we have got absolute visual proof that we don't die when our body stops working. I've searched extensively to see if what Roger has done has been done before: It hasn't. Roger's message will change all of our lives, forever.

I never expected to witness what Roger has done, and continues to do; to see such ground-breaking evidence as he has given and is still giving to us, his family, to pass on, to spread the word. Roger has co-opted me onto his team. I didn't really have much choice: He would often hand me a project, maybe changing all his lightbulbs to LEDs, replacing the kitchen hob, or in this case, relaying his message to the world that there is life after death. No pressure then, Roger! He and I are partners – him without a body in the spirit world; me still living here on Earth. Between the two of us, we are going to prove to everyone that life continues after we lose our human body.

I really am in awe of what Roger is doing, to take the steps he's taken, to make such an effort to show himself to us, when many other deceased relatives have died and haven't shown themselves to us at all. So, who *was* Roger? More accurately, who *is* Roger?

He was born in Somerset in 1936, his younger brother following a few years later. His parents were staunch Jehovah's Witnesses, so inevitably the boys were too. He grew up during the Second World War, with all the difficulties that entailed. His street was bombed, but luckily the family were unscathed.

He passed his 11-plus exam, so went to the boys-only grammar school. On reaching the Sixth Form, Roger was transformed from an average plodder into an enthusiastic searcher after knowledge.

Initially he studied the Sciences, but realised his heart lay in the Arts, so he ditched Physics and Chemistry for French, English and History, catching up on Latin in his own time.

He excelled in his A Levels and was offered a place at Lincoln College, Oxford, to study English Language and Literature.

Before he could study at Oxford, he had to deal with National Service, the 18 months of peace time conscription to the armed forces. However, Roger successfully proved to the local judge that he was a Conscientious Objector (one who is opposed to serving in the armed forces and/or bearing arms on the grounds of moral or religious principles) so was able to work in a hospital initially, before transferring to agricultural work. During this period, he met and fell in love with Joan. She too was a Jehovah's Witness, and she would later accompany Roger to Oxford once they were married.

At Oxford, he threw himself into his studies. Roger did well with his course work but felt his limited childhood education meant he didn't make the most of what university life had to offer. It was this realisation that made Roger decide to concentrate on teaching as a career, once he'd got his degree. He wanted to inspire children of the value of education and learning.

In the second year of his degree course, 1958, he and Joan got married.

His first job as a graduate was at a grammar school, teaching English. After a stint at a Bristol school, Roger got a university job in Reading. Roger and Joan by that time had a family and lived on campus in the flat that was offered as part of Roger's responsibilities as warden.

In 1970 Roger brought his family to Leeds, where he taught at university, developing in-service training for teachers.

Roger and Joan bought their first house there, where the family would live for the next twelve years. Climbing the promotional ladder, Roger changed jobs a few times, often working away from home during the week. Once Roger's working life was permanently based in and around London, he and Joan moved nearby in 1980, where they would spend the next twenty years. Their daughters were both by now rooted in Leeds, but the family met up regularly in spite of the distance.

In 1999 Roger retired after having had some major heart problems, from which he had successfully recovered. He was approaching his sixty-fifth birthday. Sadly, he felt his career had petered out at the end, rather than ending with a flourish.

Looking ahead to his retirement years, Roger moved back to Yorkshire with Joan, to be near their daughters. They chose an ideal place where there could be perfect transport links to anywhere in the country, but a small enough town for Roger to have a massive input. They joined their local Civic Society, and Roger worked tirelessly to initiate many schemes. After a few years, he was elected Chairman. His charity work blossomed, having set up a successful group for active retired people to further their learning. Eventually this group would have more than 400 members.

I first met Joan and Roger soon after I met their eldest, Caroline, my future wife, in 1978, at the sixth form disco at her school in Leeds, effectively on a blind date. I was brought up Roman Catholic, as my father was Catholic, but my mother wasn't. I went to an all-boys Catholic grammar school, so I hadn't really met many girls at all. Caroline went to a local secondary school, also attended by my mother's friend's daughter, Fiona. Mum, and Fiona's mother, were trying to get the two of us together; we got on okay, but we didn't see each other as potential partners. Fiona invited me to a disco at Roundhay School. I said yes, on condition Fiona could get a ticket for my best friend, Paul. I got a phone call out of the blue from someone called Caroline; she had some spare tickets, and she would meet us at the door. Caroline and I hit it off straight away. We have been together ever since and celebrated our fortieth wedding anniversary in 2022.

I was brought up Catholic, but once I became a teenager, I didn't really believe in it anymore. My father would take us all to church each week on Sunday mornings, my two older brothers and me, but we just went through the motions of saying our prayers, and hymns were sung, or more accurately, barely mumbled. However, in my teens, I had stopped going to church and no longer believed in Catholicism. Eventually Dad ended up going to church alone: I never really knew if he did believe in it all, or if he was just carrying on a lifelong habit. I was never sure what his true beliefs were, but regrettably I never bothered to ask him.

Caroline's parents had moved down south, near to London, for Roger's work in 1980. A year after we married, we decided to move there too, living with them for a couple of months while we house hunted. I got to know Joan and Roger even better than I had previously. My parents had moved abroad, to South Africa, so I really appreciated my in-laws – it was like having another set of parents.

Time passed, our family expanded, by 1994 we had five children and were living back in Leeds. My parents were back from South Africa, living in Bromsgrove near my older brother. I lost my dad the Christmas of that year, coincidentally just two days after Caroline's grandad died.

Stupidly, I hadn't realised how ill Dad was. When we talked on the phone I would always try and be upbeat, which may not have been quite the right thing. I was mistakenly thinking he was in better health than he was. Optimism was blinding me to the reality of the situation and he probably didn't want to scare me by telling me how ill he really was.

The day after Boxing Day my brother Tony called to say Dad had been taken to hospital and we should go down and see him. It just hadn't clicked in my mind, that this was my dad about to leave this Earth. My other brother lived nearby, so we drove down together. We just didn't go quickly enough; in fact, we stupidly had a leisurely drive down there. By the time we got there, Dad had died. It was such a shock to me. Nothing had prepared me for losing my dad, and I simply went to pieces. When I saw Dad, dead, on his bed in the hospital, because I didn't believe in an afterlife, I just saw a dead body. I knew this body had been my dad, but the grief hit me hard. I held his hands, but he was cold, grey, and it was impossible to compute that my once-living, breathing, parent had gone, and that was the end of everything for him.

I was there when Caroline's gran passed a few years later. Gwen just slipped away quietly, in her own bed with us beside her. After she died, we sat on her bed with her carers, drinking tea, reminiscing about happy times, including her in the conversation.

It was different with my mum, who had been diagnosed with dementia. She came to live with us so we could help her. At first, she was still talking, and able to walk upstairs, in good health, but as time went on her condition deteriorated, and eventually Mum had to go into a care home. In all honesty, that was the best place for her; she had all the help, attention and care she needed. It was still really difficult having a relative with dementia. As many of you will know, one of the hardest things to cope with in life is when the essence of the person you know is deteriorating daily. Her mind just disappeared in the end. Mum, as a person, just receded, until finally this person in front of us was no longer Mum. Communication is almost impossible when someone with dementia can't talk; all you can do is smile, and make the odd sign, but it's just infinitely frustrating for both of you. When Mum died due to her dementia, she hadn't been able to talk for some time, and could no longer move. The care home staff had thought she would pass away quickly because she had stopped eating and drinking, but her heart and body were strong and her death seemed to go on for days. She clung to life even though I was sure she was more than ready to go.

The strangest thing happened on her last day alive. There were several of us around her bed, when suddenly she spoke a totally lucid sentence. She hadn't spoken for many months – if not years! In a commanding voice she said, "Can you move away from the bed, you're too close." Having not spoken for so long, she suddenly said something totally sensible and coherent; it was almost miraculous.

A year later, 2017, Caroline's mum, Joan, died suddenly, without warning, at her home in Howden in East Yorkshire, where they had retired once Roger finished work.

Roger called about 10 o' clock at night to say he thought Joan had *gone*. We rushed over from Leeds, battling closed motorways and freezing temperatures; we just wanted to get there as quickly as we could, to support Roger.

An ambulance had arrived, but there was nothing they could do, she was already dead, having died instantly from a heart attack. For the person concerned, dying in that manner is probably the ideal way to go; no suffering – just there one minute, gone the next. The police were called because it was an unexpected death, and for us it was the most brutal shock. We couldn't believe it, even though we do know death does come to us all eventually.

Once again, we had experienced a relative dying.

However, most unexpectedly, within days of Joan's passing, we started to experience very strange happenings. We had televisions in the house that switched on by themselves. We had bedside lights coming on during the night by themselves. The smell of her perfume lingering in the living room. The strangest incident, to my mind, happened three days after Joan died. We were walking around Sandal Castle in Wakefield, with our dog, Poppy. We walked around the high earth mound which surrounds the castle. Halfway down, in a small tree, I noticed a bird of prey, perched. I decided to walk towards the bird to get a better look, to see what sort of bird it was. As I approached, it flew out of the tree towards us, and circled us closely, twice, at low level, before flying back to the tree, where it perched again.

That is definitely not the normal behaviour of a wild bird. I could see the bird was a female kestrel, a smallish bird of prey; it certainly hadn't been eyeing up our pet spaniel, because she would have been at least sixty times heavier than the bird. There was no way it would have been able to fly off with Poppy in its beak!

These experiences were the first time any of our relatives had given us any signs at all after they had died. Over the next few weeks and months, we had a lot of similar activity. We found it very comforting, and in an attempt to comfort Roger, we told him about the events we were attributing to Joan. He didn't comment, he didn't even acknowledge what we were telling him, and he certainly didn't agree that they were signs from Joan. I think he thought we were totally bonkers.

Joan's death was a big shock that took some reconciling on everyone's part. When she died, her dying was definitely not in the script. It had always seemed that Roger would be the one who would go first, with his long list of medical problems, each of which he had successfully battled. I had been certain that when the end came, Roger would be out the door first. He used to say he "wouldn't make old bones". His own father had died at the age of 62. Although Joan had some age-related medical issues, it did seem hers were less severe, less life-threatening. She was 86 when she died.

Roger dealt with the shock of Joan's death by throwing himself more fully into all his interests and hobbies. He went on various cruises, both unaccompanied and with friends. He had a myriad of plans, many of which he carried out. He had always been a supremely positive, active person, putting us to shame with his constant adventuring.

He always had a positive zest for life. Joan had been less mobile in her later years, so when she died it gave Roger the freedom to explore and do the things they had been unable to do for the last year or two.

Following Joan's death, we decided we would sell up our business in Leeds, and move over to be nearer Roger, to keep him company. To be honest, he didn't really need us just then, but losing Joan hit us hard and whether he liked it or not, we were going to spend more time with him, when he wasn't away enjoying his freedom!

We had come to realise life is short. The business was a massive millstone giving us no flexibility, and in our late 50s, we realised we could semi-retire by buying a cheaper house near Roger and then we would only need to work part-time. It would give us a much better work/life balance.

Roger was very excited and became our guide to the local area while we worked out what we wanted. Although Joan and Roger had lived in Howden for many years, we were not that familiar with the immediate area, so we investigated it in more detail, eventually buying a house in Goole, which was just 10 minutes' drive from him.

Roger lent us the money to buy the house, even before we had sold our house and business in Leeds. Once the sale had gone through, we paid Roger back and at last we could enjoy the semi-retirement near Roger that we had planned. All the pieces of the puzzle had finally fallen into place…

A couple of months later, all the pieces of the puzzle were thrown up in the air again, when COVID-19 struck.

It became serious, and we had our first lockdown in March 2020. We kept our sanity by taking Poppy for a long walk each day. Government guidelines (or was it the law?) said this was permissible. We would call in on Roger, to take a little shopping and to have a chat, sometimes sneaking a cup of coffee in the garden with him. Luckily the weather was fabulous. I know some sticklers for the rules would have frowned upon us, but life-and-death isn't just about food and drink, and not catching the disease. It's also about staying sane, not having a mental breakdown because you're imprisoned by your own government.

As the rules relaxed, we planned a big family get-together for the summer; all our children and grandchildren, as well as Alison and Colin's family. We arranged to hire a room in a local hall, organised music, food, a magician, a bouncy castle, and Roger was going to take centre stage at the event. The cousins would meet for the first time since they were children; it would be a post-pandemic celebration, and we planned it down to the very last little detail…

Unfortunately, another lockdown prevented it from happening, so the plans were put on ice, to be resurrected at a later date.

However, Roger's medical issues surfaced again, and in the spring of 2021, we had to forcefully persuade Roger to go to hospital, as an emergency. He had shown us an abscess that he had on his stomach, the severity of which took us all by surprise. His local doctor had seen it, and prescribed antibiotics, assuming it was just some trivial little blemish on his skin. Their advice to him was to take the antibiotics, but, if over the weekend his condition worsened, then he should take himself to the local hospital. (Local, in this case, is 40 miles away, one of the costs of living in a rural area.) Being in his 80s, and it being a weekend, the chances of him noticing that he was worse, and getting himself to the hospital, were pretty slim to non-existent.

Reading up about the problem, I realised it was potentially a matter of life and death. Eventually, after a few very bad-tempered discussions with us and Alison and her husband, Colin, we persuaded Roger he had to go to Scunthorpe Hospital, the local Accident and Emergency. To say he was very reluctant is an understatement.

Caroline took him to A&E. He was in hospital for two weeks while they treated the abscess. His diabetes and heart problems caused trouble, but he was finally allowed home. However, he just didn't heal, and he still felt so poorly. He told us he hadn't felt well for many weeks, although he couldn't put his finger on what exactly felt wrong. He said he "had just felt a bit off since Christmas".

The GP obviously hadn't picked up on it at all, and it was not until they were pressured by Caroline and Alison that they agreed to refer him back to the hospital. Roger started weekly checkups, and eventually the doctors realised that his bowel was leaking its contents into his body – this had caused the abscess in the first place. It was very serious. A second operation was required.

Roger ended up being in Scunthorpe Hospital for many weeks. The emergency surgery he needed to keep him alive was extremely complex and dangerous for a man aged 84 in poor health. His amazing surgeon operated, starting at 9 o'clock in the evening, finishing after midnight. She rang Caroline at 2 a.m., explaining exactly what she'd found. She apologised for calling in the middle of the night, but she knew we would want to know how he was.

Roger was in hospital for 71 days.

It transpired that the bowel had started leaking some months before, after some mesh had been inserted on the outside of the bowel, during a previous cancer operation to remove his spleen. The mesh had degraded and then the leak had caused the abscess. The surgeon had to insert a stoma and remove the damaged section of bowel.

Roger came home from hospital in the early summer, but he just couldn't manage with the stoma. It was constantly leaking, but more significantly than that, he just couldn't get the food intake he required in order to live, and whatever was tried, the stoma just didn't work for Roger.

His other health issues such as low blood pressure, heart failure and kidney problems, and the diabetes also started to seriously impact his life. Luckily, thanks to the amazing care he received from the team at the hospital, a few months later he was strong and healthy enough to have the stoma reversed.

The procedure was successful, but by this time his various health issues were conflicting with each other, and whatever was done he was unable to stay on an even keel. When one problem was sorted, it created another problem, and the seesaw effect just couldn't be stabilised.

Roger remained incredibly positive; he still had big plans for when he had recovered. The main plan was that he and Caroline would go back to Weston-Super-Mare in the spring, to visit family and friends still living there, and to see where he had lived in his younger days.

He still had a huge zest for life and really didn't contemplate his life ending anytime soon.

The last few days of Roger's life were during Easter, 2022. He was back in Scunthorpe Hospital.

Roger had rung Caroline at the crack of dawn, on both the Saturday and the Sunday, in a heated state, rather agitated, asking her to get down there as soon as possible. He needed something seemingly trivial, very urgently.

On Easter Monday, mid-morning, a nurse rang Caroline, telling her she might want to come down. She said Roger was not engaging or chatting, as he had the day before. She said, "He might be tired, come when you like."

There appeared to be no sense of urgency: Caroline was not alarmed, but decided she would go so she could relax later. I actually told Caroline not to bother; it didn't sound like there was a big problem, and our youngest son, Patrick, was coming for lunch, so it was an inconvenience if she went.

Thankfully Caroline ignored me, she did go to the hospital, arriving there around midday. Roger was gasping to breathe; his eyes were open, but he did not seem to be able to see. He didn't acknowledge Caroline, but his grip tightened when she took his hand. He couldn't talk. The doctor came very quickly to see Caroline; he must have been waiting for her. He explained that Roger was very ill and if it was required, they wouldn't be able to resuscitate him; it would be very invasive, his body was too weak to survive.

Roger had always wanted all the interventions possible – he had wanted whatever it took to keep him alive. Caroline felt so guilty, but had to agree with the doctor; he wouldn't be resuscitated. Just a few minutes later Roger died, Caroline holding his hand.

When she rang me soon after, I had never expected her to tell me that he had gone. I was expecting her to tell me something quite minor. Alison and Colin came to collect me and we joined Caroline at the hospital.

We sat with Roger in the room for some time. We were all in shock. Even though he had been so ill, we were not prepared for his death. Finally, Roger's previous invincibility had deserted him.

Chapter 1

Joan's and Roger's Spirits on Camera

Three weeks after Roger died, Caroline, Alison, Colin and myself went to a Stephen Holbrook evening – Stephen Holbrook is the UK's premier psychic medium.

We had seen him before, more than once. I had been planning that we would go anyway, even before Roger had died. Now it seemed like a good idea to go and see if Roger would send us a message via Stephen.

Roger came through Stephen with an amazing message which was 100% accurate.

Unfortunately, we didn't record the evening's performance, but later, between us all, retrospectively, we were able to piece together what was said. Roger was reassuring us that he wasn't in pain when he died; it was very peaceful for him; where he was now was perfect; he was very worried about three climbing plants that he had just bought and were still in his hallway when he left in the ambulance. He wanted us to make sure they would be planted and looked after. Later we found the plants, took them home and planted them. They are all doing very well. Isn't it bizarre how something so ordinary and mundane could be at the forefront of a spirit's thoughts?

Stephen explained that Roger knew that the four of us had been with him in the hospital room once he had passed, and described how Alison had kissed him goodbye, which made a big impression on him (she hadn't kissed him for two years due to the various COVID-19 official guidance/restrictions/laws/whatever).

We first heard about Stephen Holbrook from Colin, who had been to see him a few years previously, following the death of his father, Alec, in 2009. He had seen an advert in the local paper for a Stephen Holbrook evening and felt the information had leapt out of the page, convincing him he needed to go, which he did.

His father came through with a message and was very forceful. Stephen said he had someone pushing in, and that was exactly how Alec's character was: determined to be heard. Stephen asked if the date of 23 February meant anything to anyone. Initially, Colin had remained quiet as he mistakenly thought his dad's birthday was 22 February, however, Stephen was very insistent that it was the twenty-third. Later Colin checked with his mother, Ada; she confirmed that his dad's birthday was indeed on the twenty-third.

A few months later, Colin took Roger to see Stephen Holbrook because he had been interested in Colin's experience and was keen to see him for himself. Again, Colin's dad came through during the show. Initially Roger had seemed reasonably impressed, but later, on the way home in the car, he changed his mind, telling Colin that the messages were a bit vague. Seemingly, Roger was not convinced of either Stephen Holbrook's psychic abilities, or the afterlife, after all.

After Roger died, Caroline and I regularly visited the cemetery where he was to be buried next to his wife, Joan. We had been frequent visitors before, paying our respects to Joan since she died four years previously. We hadn't witnessed anything out of the ordinary with Joan at the cemetery, and the signs she had given us previously had diminished. We had seen Stephen Holbrook a couple of times in the hope Joan might come through with a message, but we had never heard anything from her.

We had visited the cemetery the day Roger died and continued to call in regularly over the following days, planning how we were going to organise the graves. The headstone had to be removed for the burial and then would be sent back to the monumental masons for the additional wording to be added.

We also decided to have a photograph of Joan and Roger etched onto the back of the stone. We had plenty of time to decide and implement the plans, as the headstone couldn't be replaced for six months from Roger's burial. For us it was an excellent reason to regularly visit the cemetery, and other local cemeteries, getting ideas from the other headstones and graves, and investigating what was possible. We enjoyed the peace and serenity of the cemetery, and it gave our now very elderly spaniel the opportunity of a very gentle walk. Strictly speaking, dogs aren't allowed in the cemetery, but we kept our fingers crossed that none of the other spirits there would grass us up to the authorities – to date, it seems no spirits have reported us!

When we went to the grave, Caroline or I would take video film on the mobile phone, so we had a record of our visits, the grave, and the surroundings. This was to help us formulate the plans for what we wanted to be done.

While I was reviewing this footage, incredibly, I started to see various light anomalies on the film. Some of them were hard to spot, and it required concentrated examination of the footage. But some of them were surprisingly easy to notice. One of the most impressive happened literally just a couple of days after Roger died. At the grave there were dozens of little light anomalies, initially seeming like lots of insects flying around, but when you study them very closely, you can see that they aren't insects. They are little specks of light moving around.

I'm still not sure exactly what the light anomalies are, but they are definitely something to do with the spirits. Whether each spirit has one light anomaly they are able to control, or whether one spirit can create many light anomalies, I am not certain.

After seeing these bizarre light anomalies, we took even more video footage, and I would regularly check it when we got home for future reference.

Roger has given us a few signs since he died, but nowhere near as many as Joan had given when she died. We have had one or two strange electrical problems in the house with the lights that I haven't been able to explain. I put those down to Roger. My mobile phone crashed two days after Roger died. I had to reset it. It had never done that before. It's never done it since. When Caroline had owned it before me, it had never done it, so I also attribute that to Roger.

Once, when Caroline was on a call discussing an offer for Roger's house with the estate agents, the phone line went haywire, making strange other-worldly noises that the agent described as "spooky". Again, we put that down to Roger. Possibly the most bizarre of all was a few weeks after Roger died, Caroline was at work and the virtual assistant was playing *Hits of the 80s*. She was talking to a colleague about the funeral, when all of a sudden, the song, "The First Time Ever I Saw Your Face", sung by Roberta Flack, started to play. This is the song that Roger chose to play at Joan's funeral, and Caroline and Alison also chose it for Roger's funeral. There is no doubt this was Roger playing the song, as it definitely *wasn't* a hit of the '80s.

The headstone was moved, and over the next few days we were able to finish off the grave for Joan and Roger. We installed low cast-iron edging around the perimeter, having levelled the soil, and then we covered the plot in slate chippings. The plot is very tightly situated between neighbouring graves, so the accuracy of the position of the headstone and edging was paramount. It has worked brilliantly and we are all delighted with the end result.

We visit the grave to pay our respects and to admire it, and to speak to Roger, to see if he likes having the best grave in the cemetery. I get the feeling that he approves, as we continued to see light anomalies on film when we reviewed the footage.

On bonfire night in 2022, Alison suggested that we go to the cemetery to let off some fireworks that she had found at Roger's house, while clearing out his effects. The rockets were many years old, having been forgotten at the back of the garage, but she thought it would be nice to set them off in memory of relatives who had died. We had a couple of our grandchildren staying with us, and Caroline was worried they may be a bit scared going to the cemetery in the dark, but they were just excited.

We hadn't been to the cemetery at night before but armed with a torch each, we had enough light to see where we were going. It was a lovely evening and the visit was surprisingly enjoyable. We found the cemetery very calming, serene and very beautiful. Many of the graves were lit with solar powered lights – it was not scary at all. I filmed as usual and checked it later. Some light anomalies were present again. You have to look very carefully to tell what is a light anomaly and what is an ordinary speck of light, either from fireworks, or reflections from a torch playing tricks with the camera lens, but there were definitely some light anomalies on camera.

After the visit we decided that we would add some lights to her parents' grave. Caroline wanted some sort of battery-powered lantern, and I suggested that we also have a battery-powered LED spotlight shining on the engraving of Joan and Roger which had been etched onto the rear of the headstone. I worked out a way to do this using rechargeable batteries which would be housed in a graveside vase, with wires buried under the slate chippings. I installed it a week or two later, and we are delighted with the result. We visit weekly to replace the batteries. We know that Roger approves as when we go to the cemetery, we sometimes see light anomalies at their graveside.

After seeing my obsession with the light anomalies on video, Caroline suggested that I might want to investigate further, and suggested I should buy some of the equipment I had seen on the ghost hunting programmes I had been watching. Not only had I been watching the programmes on TV, I had also read dozens of books on the topic, as well as the wider subject of how ghosts and spirits occur; indeed, everything paranormal.

In doing my homework on the subject, I had watched hundreds of episodes of ghost hunting programmes. I had become familiar with the equipment, how it is used, and I could see that it could work very well. I told Caroline that I wouldn't want to do ghost hunting myself, because I would be petrified. Doing it at night, in the pitch black, would be scary, and also, I would be frightened of attracting evil spirits, which does seem to be a very real danger. I also just couldn't see the attraction of hunting for the spirits of people I had never known.

After a lot of consideration and research, I decided that if I could get some equipment to search for the spirit of Roger, that would be both fascinating and an amazing challenge that I was now keen to embark on.

Initially I decided to buy an EMF meter, which is widely accepted to indicate the presence of a spirit.

What happened next is totally incredible, almost unbelievable.

Everything in this book really happened. I still have to pinch myself because it is all so amazing. It still hasn't fully sunk in yet; the lengths Roger has gone to in order to let us know he is still around!

The next few chapters explain how everything unfolded.

I never planned to write a book, but what Roger has done has meant I had no other option, if I was to spread his message to the world, which is evidently what Roger wants me to do.

Roger co-opted me onto his team for a reason, and that reason is to tell the world that there *is* life after death.

When Roger was alive as a physical human being, he was adamant that there was *no* afterlife. Every time I tried to talk to him about it, he would just say, "There is no life after death, that's it!"

This explains why he was so keen to live. What Roger has found since his body died is evidently not what he was expecting at all. He has had such a shock that he is bending over backwards to tell us, to tell the world, that things aren't how he thought they were.

We are all incredibly privileged that Roger has set himself on this mission, to tell us all how it really is.

It's up to us all to listen to his message, and to value his first-hand account of what happens when we lose our physical body.

I hope everyone who reads this book will realise what an incredible person Roger is. He was a passionate believer in education and communication. As a spirit Roger has exactly the same personality he had when he was physically living on Earth. Apart from reading all about him, and what he has done, he has proved there is an afterlife, on camera.

For the first time ever in human history, we now have incontrovertible proof of what awaits us all.

Watch the video for the first chapter to see for yourself what Roger and Joan have shown us, on camera. I'm sure it will amaze you, as it still amazes us. What you are seeing on the video is a green stick figure wherever the special SLS camera detects a spirit – later chapters explain in detail the way the equipment works.

Any of you reading this book who would like to try and see your late loved ones on camera, might like to try something similar to what we did. I wish you all the luck in the world – it really is something very, very special, and priceless. It's definitely been worth all the effort.

Chapter 2

Joan's and Roger's Signs from the Afterlife

In the previous chapter you have seen how Roger appeared, unbelievably, on camera, when I first tried out the new equipment at the cemetery for the very first time. Equally unbelievably, a couple of days later when Caroline came with me to the cemetery, to see me using the SLS camera in order to see if her dad would show up again, Roger did show up, and after a little while, so did Joan. I had asked Roger the first time if he could try and bring Joan to see us when I returned with Caroline, and amazingly, she did come too.

I need to tell you how we got to this stage; how did we suspect that it might even be possible, even though it would be a very long shot, to see Joan and Roger on camera?

Well, Joan died over four years before Roger. She died without any warning, very suddenly. She died at home in the living room with Roger, just the two of them in the house, December 2017. She was just getting up out of her chair when she collapsed on the floor. She had no chance to say anything. This was the most sudden and brutal shock for Roger, his lifelong partner there one minute, gone the next. Roger always told me that there was no afterlife, although Caroline wonders if he didn't truly believe that – maybe, she thinks, he might have secretly believed in it.

Did Joan believe in an afterlife? I think she did. She still had leanings towards her religion from her earlier years, when she and Roger were committed Jehovah's Witnesses. Even though Roger had given up on religion, in spite of searching for the right religion for him, Joan still believed in her religious upbringing.

When Joan died so suddenly, she must have been as shocked as Roger was. She hadn't had a chance to say goodbye – to anyone! Knowing what we now know, that there really is an afterlife, Joan must have been totally at a loss to know what comes next. She will have been there in spirit, seeing her own body on the living room floor, Roger inconsolable, the ambulance paramedics checking, but totally unable to revive her. When Caroline and I arrived about an hour after she died, after a horrendous journey in the very late evening, we could only try and give Roger some moral support, while we spoke to Joan, lifeless on the floor, the police and ambulance people doing their duties. Caroline's sister, Alison, and her husband, Colin, were there, and the five of us tried to take in what had just happened. The great comfort for all of us was that she went instantly, no suffering, no time to suffer, and the ambulance came very quickly (which they don't always). Joan had died as painlessly as is possible, which surely is what we would all choose for ourselves?

Poor Joan will have been watching us all, beside ourselves with grief, unable to talk to any of us, wanting to console us as we registered what her lifeless body signified. I had always suspected Roger would die before Joan, and I think both of them probably thought that too. Here were her husband and her daughters totally bereft, and she couldn't do anything to help them – *or could she?*

In the next day or two, Joan started to give Caroline and me signs that she was still around. Initially we just thought one of the televisions in our house had gone faulty, turning itself on. Very soon we realised that it wasn't faulty – Joan was sending us a message.

It wasn't just one television, it was all three of them, at various times. One of our bedside lights turned itself on at four o'clock in the morning, while we were both deeply asleep. That was a very big shock, but also very lovely and reassuring – as soon as we realised – yes, this really is Joan sending us messages, and we are very happy to have her send them to us. Some people find this sort of thing frightening and disturbing, but we just welcomed it with open arms.

Just to prove to us that it really was Joan sending us these signs, Caroline smelt Joan's favourite perfume in our house – an unambiguous sign – Joan couldn't be clearer.

My favourite sign that Joan gave us in the days after she died was while we were walking at Sandal Castle near where we lived. Caroline and I were walking Poppy our beloved spaniel around the grassy mound which surrounds the ancient castle ruins. On the grassy slope there was a small tree below where we were walking, and in the branches of the tree I could see a bird of prey, perched. I said to Caroline that I was going to walk down closer to the tree to try and see what type of bird it was. As I started approaching the bird, it flew out of the tree and approached the three of us. It circled us at low level, just above our head height, twice, in tight circles, then back to the tree, to perch back where it had come from.

The video linked to this chapter shows a still photo of this actual bird, which was a female kestrel.

Feathers appearing in impossible to explain places are one of the most recognised signs of a spirit sending a message to a loved one – we got lots of those. Sometimes a feather would appear in the house, all the windows shut, really no conventional explanation – we knew these were Joan effectively talking to us. We still get them occasionally even now, over six years since she died. They always bring a smile to our faces.

Butterflies, too, are another most popular and widely acknowledged sign from a spirit – again, we have had lots of these, sometimes in the house, but mainly outside. It's something about the behaviour of the butterfly that gives the game away – an unnatural propensity to stay close to us.

The very best butterfly sign happened just a few months ago, years after Joan died. It could have been a sign from Roger, but our instincts tell us that Joan is the butterfly specialist. We had gone to Joan and Roger's cemetery for our regular weekly visit, and Caroline and I were talking about signs, particularly butterfly signs. Just that morning, before we went out, we had watched an episode of a Netflix series, *Surviving Death*. The episode was one I had already seen, which I wanted Caroline to see, as this episode was all about signs – some were very impressive butterfly appearances.

We were talking about Joan revealing butterflies to us, and we were including Joan in the conversation, saying to her how impressed we were with her signs. As we walked back through the cemetery after visiting the grave, Caroline suddenly noticed lots of the same species of butterfly, Red Admirals, all perched in various places. There were many on three adjacent gravestones, then we noticed at least a dozen or more in a nearby bush in the hedgerow. There must have been at least thirty altogether – we couldn't count them all. Caroline managed to photograph some of the ones on the gravestones, then within a minute or two they had all gone. We've never seen butterflies in these numbers before, or since.

This was definitely Joan's coup de grace – so totally, incredibly impressive, the most relevant possible message to us relating to the conversation we'd just had with her!

On the video for this chapter there is a still photo of some of the butterflies we actually saw.

Another strange anomaly on camera, which happened a couple of years after Joan died, but before Roger died, was a video Caroline took at our local cemetery (not the one where Joan is buried), when we were walking Poppy. Caroline spotted a blackbird bathing in the water in a headstone, which was a lovely sight. When she reviewed the footage, Caroline saw a strange light on the grass in front of the headstone, which initially we thought was supernatural. It was this light effect that made us decide to video regularly whenever we were at Joan's cemetery, or anywhere else where we suspected something strange might show on camera. Even though in retrospect this light feature wasn't anything paranormal, but merely internal camera reflections from a bright reflection off a distant gravestone in view, this decision proved a very wise move. It made us study all our videos very carefully every time, revealing several very strange, genuinely paranormal light anomalies.

To anyone intrigued by the possibility of their relative giving them a message in some form or other, I would advise you to use your smartphone to film every time you might spot something interesting, then study it carefully. Modern digital cameras (phones are what most of us use as cameras) are very receptive to showing various light anomalies which are unseen by the naked eye. Some anomalies are visible to the naked eye – we have both seen one or two, but people like us with no great psychic ability often don't see anything, whereas the phone will. Also, if something happens, but you never recorded it, you'll be kicking yourself later.

The video for this chapter shows the blackbird footage.

I have since read about animals giving us signs from departed spirits, so I know the amazing kestrel sign was Joan sending us the most incredible message of all. I have been a lifelong bird enthusiast, so I appreciated this sign more than any others Joan sent. Making electronic equipment do something unexpected is definitely most impressive, but making a wild creature do something it would never normally do – to me, that's in another league. Thanks, Joan!

When we told Roger, Alison and Colin about these various signs, they seemed sceptical, to put it mildly. I think they thought we were cracking up, imagining things that weren't real, certainly not anything to do with recently deceased Joan. Roger wouldn't even comment on our signs – uncharacteristically at a loss for words. Maybe he was just too confused with the whole business to know what to say – remember, this was Roger, the avowed non-believer of life after death.

Colin did believe in life after death, in some form or other, as he had recommended Stephen Holbrook, the top UK medium, who came through with a message from Colin's dad at one of his shows that Colin felt compelled to attend, very shortly after his dad had died. Colin was so impressed; the message was so spot on.

Caroline and I, between us, had had many relatives die over the years, pretty inevitably, as we were in our late fifties, but we had never had anyone give us any signs after they died, that we were aware of. This time, with Joan, things were different – she sent us signs, and we welcomed them.

From all the books I've read, it seems that if you open yourself up to the spirits getting in touch, they will keep trying to communicate. This, I believe, is why Joan picked us (the others didn't get any signs, so they said).

Looking back, I think maybe the crucial difference with Joan was that she died so abruptly. With most deaths there is some warning, so both the dying and the remaining family have time to say their goodbyes. They die with no unfinished business.

Joan died without that time to say goodbye, so once her spirit was discarnate, she had a compulsion to talk to us somehow. I've read that people who die suddenly sometimes don't even know they're dead – how sad and weird when you think about that! Is it really possible? Maybe it is.

How do we explain the signs Roger gave us when he died four years after Joan, bearing in mind that he apparently didn't believe in an afterlife?

Well, that non-belief is the very reason he has given us his signs and impelled us to get equipment to try and communicate with him. As in their life before death, what Joan started, Roger has taken over. Joan sent her signs to Caroline and me (which Roger didn't believe), then once he died and was also a discarnate spirit, he found that, actually, there IS life after death, so he took over Joan's quest and tried to get our attention, which obviously he has succeeded in.

Roger knew Caroline and I were open to everything supernatural, paranormal, so from his vantage point he embarked on his mission to get our attention, and get his message across to both of us and the wider world. Roger was an educator in life, and in the afterlife, he is still an educator. The one thing we take with us when we die is knowledge. Everything we knew in life we also know in the afterlife. We have the same personality as we did, the only difference is we don't have a physical body anymore.

Joan's and Roger's bodies now lie underground, decomposing, but Joan and Roger as people are still around us, minus their bodies, as spirits. If we listen to their messages, they will talk to us – not physically, but via dreams and physical messages, and psychically, if we can tune in as mediums do.

The books I've read say that we can all develop our psychic abilities, by being open and trusting our instincts. We're still trying but have a long way to go.

Roger knows we aren't psychics yet, but he always loved gadgets, so it's totally appropriate that he has impelled me to get various electronic devices for him to communicate with us. In a later chapter I will describe in detail the equipment we got, and how it works. You can see for yourself on the videos how Roger shows up on the SLS camera as a stick figure. Anyone who is sceptical can read in a later chapter, (about the Society for Psychical Research) how it was proved that this camera really was seeing a spirit – it wasn't being falsely triggered by items or features in shot, which is what the sceptics say is the explanation for these cameras seeing a stick figure that is not superimposed onto a living human (which is what the cameras were designed to do).

Again, the decision to video everything has paid off. Every time I use the SLS camera, I video it with my smartphone. I now have well over a hundred videos, all with Roger, and sometimes Joan, showing up. Sometimes it takes a while for Roger to show up, as long as half an hour, but if there is a compelling reason to show, he might be there almost instantly.

So, what other signs have Joan and Roger given us?

While Roger was in hospital, in his last few months, one of many long stays he had, Caroline and her sister, Alison, were in his bedroom at home, tidying and decluttering the room, so that when he came home from hospital, he would be able to manage in the bedroom a little easier. They were feeling overwhelmed with all the drawers and cupboards in the bedroom being full of Roger's socks and other clothing. They were saying how he always took over any space, at Joan's expense.

Caroline said to Alison, "What would Mum say?" and with that, the telephone in the house gave one ring. Alison looked completely stunned, unable to speak. When they checked the phone's call log to see who had been ringing, there was no one. Joan was evidently contributing to the conversation!

Another amazing sign, just a month after Roger died, was when Caroline was at work, at an opticians in the town which overlooks the railway crossing. I was at home half a mile away, when a horse-drawn hearse and funeral cortege passed our house. I rang Caroline at work, to tell her to look out the window at work in a few minutes, to see the beautiful sight of the horse-drawn hearse.

She started talking to her colleague about her dad's funeral, while they both looked out for the cortege. The Alexa personal assistant was playing '80s music. As Caroline told her colleague about Roger's funeral, Alexa suddenly started playing the '60s song "The First Time Ever I Saw Your Face", by Roberta Flack. This very song was the song chosen to be played by Roger at both Joan's, and his own funeral.

Caroline and her colleague both dissolved into tears.

We had a number of other signs on mobile phones and TVs, electrical circuits in the house tripping out without explanation etc., after Roger died – he was very much carrying on where Joan left off!

Yet another sign from Roger was six months after he died, when the headstone which had been engraved with Roger's details was being returned and re-sited on the grave, now that Roger had joined Joan in the cemetery. Caroline and I were preparing to go to the cemetery, as we did most weeks, to measure up where exactly the headstone needed to be positioned, as the memorial company were due to come in a few days to install it. Position was critical, as neighbouring graves were very close each side of Joan and Roger's grave, and our plans for the grave fencing needed the headstone to be absolutely central on the plot.

Just before we were to leave the house, as I was sat in the living room near the electrical fuse-box, a circuit tripped out with a loud bang. I reset it and it tripped again. I could find no reason to explain it, and after the second reset it didn't trip again. Something told me I needed to collect the items I'd ordered from the local hardware shop, on the way to the cemetery.

When we got to the cemetery, we instantly saw that the memorial people had installed the headstone a few days earlier than expected, but in the wrong place. Luckily, I had collected the ground marking paint from the hardware shop, and we were able to mark the ground to show the memorial people where exactly the headstone should be sited.

A few days later the mistake was rectified. Roger had without doubt alerted me to the fact that his gravestone was in the wrong place, and that I needed the marking paint before we went to the cemetery.

Even though I never heard any words from Roger, I had a feeling, and Roger's electrical sign made sure I didn't ignore that feeling he'd given me. This is what everyone with spiritual leanings tells us – *trust your instincts and take note of any signs.*

Although I am by no means psychic, I am learning, and on all the occasions I see spirits on camera, I am trusting my instincts when I think I know that it is Roger, or possibly Joan. I know my instincts are correct, and to anyone who wants to try and do what we have done, my best advice to you is to do whatever feels right for you.

Later chapters in the book will explain just how important it is to trust your own feelings – don't believe anyone who tells you what you ought to be doing; do what you feel to be right.

On the video for this chapter, after the blackbird, is a video taken at Joan's grave days after Roger died, but before his funeral. We were there to think about how the grave was to be redone once the funeral had taken place. Roger was to be buried next to Joan, the headstone was to be taken away and replaced in six months' time (a council regulation), which actually was most helpful, as it gave us plenty of time to work out what to do to the grave.

The phone, bizarrely, decided to film at half-speed of its own accord. When I studied the footage, I couldn't quite believe what I was seeing. On the face of it, it looks as though there are some little insects flying around the grave, particularly around the planter and the potted rose. It took me a long time to appreciate this video, which requires careful study – maybe this is why Joan or Roger made the camera film at half speed, so it's more apparent to us. They are actually not insects, but little winged creatures which sometimes appear and disappear spontaneously, coming out of and going into the ground/soil. Sometimes they are light coloured, then instantly they are dark coloured, and vice versa.

There are little fly type creatures on the yellow rose, but again they appear/disappear instantly. I have since read about spirit flies and winged light anomalies. I believe these are spirits, probably the spirits of family and friends welcoming Roger to the afterlife. This is what happens according to many of the books I've read. It's all quite bizarre, beautiful and magical. This is our chance to glimpse entities from another dimension, made briefly visible for ordinary humans like us to see with our physical eyes.

Two weeks before Roger died, he told Caroline, totally matter-of-fact, that his younger brother, Tony, who predeceased him, had been in the room, sat on the settee next to him. It's very well reported and corroborated that spirits of relatives do indeed come and greet us some days or weeks before we die.

When Caroline told me this at the time, I said to her, "I wonder if that means your dad has only a few weeks left to live?" It proved to be prophetic, not that I'm any sort of seer, but I was merely relaying the stories I'd read in so many books on this matter, by very credible authors.

In this chapter's video, after the cemetery footage, is video Caroline took in our spare bedroom after Roger had died. She was filming to show Jo, Caroline's friend in Australia, (and the editor of this book), how I'd redone the room. We'd furnished it with several of Roger's possessions, including his TV, curtains and clock. When she reviewed the footage, there were many light anomalies flying in all directions. This appears to be a lot of spiritual activity – they are definitely not reflections in the camera etc. The video shows one light anomaly, slowed down ten times, flying across the mirror. I've also shown a still, taken from the video, of this anomaly, so you can better see it – it's a very fast anomaly, showing quite a blur on the footage.

The next segment of the video shows footage Caroline took at work, about a year after Roger died. She was drawn to look out of the window. Above the building opposite she saw lots of bright flashing lights in the sky. By the time she got her phone out and started videoing, most of the lights had stopped showing, but then this very strange, almost indescribable, light anomaly/creature, flew down from the sky at great speed, and disappeared into the brick wall of the building.

This video is also slowed down ten times, as the thing moved so quickly. I have shown a series of stills from the video so you can see the detail of it, frame by frame. It is a creature about the size of a small bird, judging from the size when it's in front of the brick wall. It has beating, luminous wings, very bright white, as if the light is illuminating them from behind. The body part is black.

What is it? It looks as though it is similar to the winged creatures at the cemetery but bigger and quicker. Maybe it is a spirit, or angel, or...

Whatever it is, something impelled Caroline to look out of the window at that moment, to see the flashing lights, then this happened.

Maybe it's Joan, or Roger, or, who knows? It's very impressive, and it certainly got Caroline's attention.

It just underlines the fact that you really need to film at all times, if you are at all interested in studying what your deceased loved one might be trying to show you. You wouldn't want to miss their messages, would you? And if you don't try and capture their messages, maybe they will stop trying to contact you. That is certainly what we take from all of this as our number one lesson.

About seven months after Roger died, I finally got my first item of ghost-hunting equipment, after Caroline kept gently nudging me to get some devices. I'd watched hundreds of ghost-hunting programmes, to see what equipment actually worked.

The last segment of the video for this chapter shows what happened when we took the K2 EMF meter to the cemetery to try it out for the first time. These devices weren't designed for ghost-hunting but were intended to be used to measure electro-magnetic fields in houses and offices and the like, to check for safe levels of electro-magnetic radiation (EMF). Literally, EMF stands for Electromotive Force. For instance, your microwave oven could be giving out dangerous levels of EMF, and this meter would tell you, by the LEDs all lighting up – the more that light up, the stronger the electric field. I will talk in more detail about all the equipment in the next chapter.

Ghost hunters found that spirits can make these devices register their electric field. The video shows us having a *conversation* with Roger, and amazingly it shows that he still has his sense of humour. A spirit, or consciousness, whatever you want to call it, has exactly the same personality as they did when they were a physical person on Earth. The only difference is that they are now discarnate, their failing physical body having *given up the ghost*.

This ancient expression literally does mean the spirit has left the body, so our forebears really did understand that spirits reside in living beings but leave the body when it physically dies. It's only in more recent times that Western cultures have forgotten what our predecessors already knew.

Back to the video for this chapter, there is footage of us using the K2 EMF meter at the cemetery for the first time: I talk to Roger about getting some more equipment from America, so we could try and see him (SLS camera) and he could talk to us using an electronic dictionary (Ovilus). He responds positively, flashing the EMF meter.

At the end of these chats we tell him we'll have to turn the meter off and go, because someone else is coming into the cemetery – we didn't want to upset anyone with our equipment – "They might think we're weirdos!" – big flash of the lights from Roger.

Chapter 3

Equipment Used to Communicate with Roger

In this chapter I will explain how we use various pieces of equipment to hunt for Roger's spirit. The most basic bit of equipment, and the one Roger used initially to alert us to the fact that he's still around after his death, is a smartphone, which you can use in camera or video mode. These days almost everyone has one of these, even people like me – a bit of a technophobe, well into my sixties. This is certainly where anyone interested in looking for their loved one should start, I suggest. As soon as we realised Roger was creating light anomalies on camera, we would record every time we went to the cemetery, and then I would check the footage to see if there were any new light anomalies. Every bit of video that had something of interest on it, we saved, and over time it became an issue of how to save all the videos in a safe and secure way. Caroline is the more tech savvy of us, so I tend to end up with her castoff iPads and iPhones, as she gets the latest model. The iPhone that I was using works well enough for me, and Caroline has been great at organising the storage of all the videos on the iCloud. This has meant that my iPad is pretty much dedicated to Roger's videos. I regularly delete any unused or unnecessary photographs that might end up on my iPad from other people, so that I've got enough memory to store all of Roger's videos very securely, without any danger of running out of memory.

As said previously, I watched hundreds of ghost hunting programmes, both English and American, and generally all the top ghost hunters in these programmes use very similar equipment, so I could be sure that if I bought the same type of equipment, then I would be in with a chance of locating, and maybe even seeing, Roger's spirit. I have also read dozens and dozens of books on the subject of not so much ghost hunting, but scientific research and theories into everything paranormal, and beyond the most conventional and mainstream science, regarding ghosts, spirits, souls and everything else related. The consensus seems to be that all spirits and ghosts are some form of electrical energy, or at least, whatever they are is very much related to electrical energy, and they have the ability to affect things electrically. This makes sense of how all this ghost hunting equipment works, and from all the programmes I have watched and still watch, I am confident that I can discriminate genuine ghost/spirit activity and activation of the various devices.

The first bit of equipment I got, after the iPhone used as a camera which I already had, was the K2 EMF meter. This is an American device, with several LEDs which light up in the presence of an electromagnetic field. It is very simple to use, but also very effective. It was designed for commercial and domestic use, to check for safe levels of EMF in buildings, particularly in the vicinity of electrical equipment such as you would find in a typical kitchen or living room, in fact any room in the house. Generally, higher EMF levels are adjacent to higher powered equipment, such as microwave ovens, as well as televisions, internet routers, etc. It is known that high levels of EMF in a building can be a health concern, so this meter allows people to check that they are living with, or working with, safe levels of EMF, or electric fields. Ghost hunters found that this device could detect spirits in the vicinity, and since buying my K2 meter, I can confirm that they definitely do work.

The K2 meter I bought was a genuine one, which only cost around £40. There are cheaper copies which look almost identical, but when I set out to buy various bits of ghost hunting equipment, I decided that if I was to stand a chance of locating Roger, I should get genuine equipment, because if this venture wasn't successful, I would never know if it was because the equipment was a cheap copy which didn't work, or whether Roger really wasn't there at all.

As soon as I tried out the EMF meter it responded very strongly when we tried it at the cemetery, as described in Chapter 1. With this simple bit of equipment, it really is possible to have a conversation with the spirit, with them making the LEDs light up in response to your questions. Anything that we asked Roger that might elicit a positive reply, Roger would light up all the LEDs into the red zone (full scale). Also, when you say something that Roger agrees with strongly, he will also light the LEDs into the red. This all assumes that Roger is around, and in the mood to talk to you. There are times when the K2 meter doesn't seem to be responding to anything, even when I know Roger is around, and maybe this is because he's just not in the mood to chat, or possibly he is unable to for some reason. Maybe his energy is depleted, or possibly there is some other explanation. Maybe eventually Roger might be able to tell us why this is the case, but for now I accept that he can activate it very strongly sometimes, and not at all at other times.

I ordered this K2 meter in November 2022, at the suggestion of Caroline. Once it had arrived and we saw just how keen Roger was to use it with us, I immediately decided that we would buy two other bits of equipment which I thought would potentially give us everything we needed to get visual evidence of Roger's spirit, and to possibly talk with him. I told Roger what we were planning to do, and he seemed very keen on the idea. When I explained to him what equipment we were going to get, he gave us very strong responses on the K2 EMF meter – he really did seem to be taking the lead in the plan for this grand experiment. Maybe I was merely just following Roger's instructions right from day one.

Even though the COVID-19 pandemic was over, there were many industries, particularly the electronics industry, which had been hit very hard, and components, and therefore the equipment that requires those components, were in very short supply. This was very evident with lots of ghost hunting equipment. The K2 meter hadn't been an issue – that was easily obtained. But I was looking to buy an Ovilus talking dictionary, which is made by a company called Digital Dowsing. These devices are renowned as being the most effective in the field of ghost hunting, and there have been a number of different models over the years. The model that everyone seems to use in the ghost hunting programmes is the Ovilus 3, which is something like 20 years old. Even though later models exist, this one seems to be the easiest to use and the most desirable. This was definitely the one I was going to get, but how would I get one when they're so rarely for sale? Looking on eBay, I could find just one or two for sale worldwide. One that was for sale was in the US, but it said they wouldn't post outside of the US. I did message the seller, but they were adamant they wouldn't post to the UK. The person selling it just happened to be Bill Chapell, the creator of the legendary Ovilus, and the man who set up and runs the company Digital Dowsing. This Ovilus 3 was from his personal collection, so it was definitely a collector's item.

I kept searching day and night for an Ovilus 3 and saw one in an auction in the US, which could be shipped to the UK. I watched this auction develop over a few days, and at 3 o'clock in the morning UK time, I managed to win the auction. Caroline paid for it straight away with PayPal, and then it was just a matter of waiting for it to be shipped to us. Total cost was £900, which I know is a lot of money, but as I've already said, we either try this quest whole-heartedly with the very best possible equipment, or there's no point trying it at all. As I told Caroline, in the worst-case scenario, if we can't find Roger with this good equipment, then we can always sell the equipment and hopefully recoup most of our money. Roger was very keen on his gadgets and technology, so it was entirely appropriate that we should try and find him using gadgets and technology. Maybe this is one of the reasons why our possibly mad quest turned out to be so successful, as Roger was doing everything he possibly could to help us find him, and for us to hear his message. He was definitely pulling our celestial strings.

The last bit of equipment I wanted to get was an SLS camera, which again I have seen on all the ghost hunting programmes. This device allows spirits to be actually seen on camera. If the camera detects an invisible spirit, the very clever technology within the camera can see that there is something there, and it puts a stick figure onto the camera image. In all the programmes, these cameras seemed to be very effective.

In case you're wondering what SLS stands for, it's Structured Light Sensor. The camera emits infrared light in a grid pattern, one million dots of light, which when they are detected by the sensor, allows the software within the camera to see the shape of the objects it is looking at. It is these infrared dots which are able to detect invisible-to-the-naked-eye spirits, by detecting a slight change in position of some of the dots. The spirit's energy, either electrical or some other form of energy, is able to displace some molecules in the air, either the air's gaseous molecules, such as oxygen (it is oxygen's ability to deflect light which creates an apparent blue sky in the atmosphere), or possibly water molecules, which are always present at some level. Water molecules have polarity (positive charge at one end, negative at the other), so are influenced by electrical fields.

The problem I had, yet again, was trying to locate a camera for sale. After looking online, I saw that an English company manufactured these cameras, so I decided to buy one of these, new. Even new SLS cameras use an obsolete Microsoft Xbox Kinect sensor, which was a device used by computer gamers some 10 or 15 years ago to play their games. As these things are no longer made, all the companies that make SLS cameras seem to use the same obsolete Microsoft SLS camera. I did find that Digital Dowsing, the makers of the Ovilus, used to make their own SLS camera, which was made from scratch using their own technology, although the prototype had used a Microsoft SLS camera. But once again, these cameras were not available – not in production anymore. I have never seen a used one of these for sale, so I suspect they must be very rare.

I ordered the English camera, and it came within a few days. I turned it on and tried it in the house, but it was very hard to use for several reasons. The software on this camera was not Microsoft software, but something else in which the view the camera saw appeared as a very, very, basic picture, comprised of blocks of solid colour on the screen. There were just a handful of colours which represented the scene the camera was looking at. So, it was very hard to determine what was what – there was absolutely no detail in the picture. On top of this basic picture, any spirit that showed up would be a stick figure. It did appear that there were some spirits in our house, but I couldn't actually relate to the picture, to know exactly where these spirits were. The biggest complication was that the picture was reversed side to side, a mirror image of the scene the camera was viewing. Everything that seemed to be on the left, according to the computer screen, was actually on the right in real-life, and vice versa. So apart from an ultra-basic picture composed of blocks of colour, it was flipped side to side as well! My brain just couldn't cope with the complexity of trying to instantaneously work out where any of these spirits were. Obviously, I'm not sure if these really were spirits, or maybe the camera was seeing things that weren't really there, but either way, it was totally unsatisfactory. I rang the company and spoke to the technical department, to say about this reversed picture, and they explained that all SLS cameras have this issue. They all show the picture reversed side to side – it's just an inherent characteristic of these gaming cameras, and there was no way they could sort it out.

Although I wasn't happy with this camera, we did take it to the cemetery to try it out, in the hope we would see Roger on camera in some form – even if we couldn't tell where he was. The day we took it, the weather was very cold, below freezing, so it was hard to use the equipment without our hands getting seriously frozen. I turned the SLS camera on, and instantly it crashed, and I could not restart it. We took it home and I tried it again in the house, but it had crashed comprehensively – nothing would get it going again. This was the final nail in the coffin for this SLS camera, so I sent it back for a refund.

The next problem facing me was how could I get an SLS camera which would hopefully work? I searched on eBay worldwide again, and saw an American company selling SLS cameras, which again were based on the Microsoft Xbox 360 sensor, but they were running a Toshiba WT8 tablet computer, and obsolete Microsoft Kinect software. The pictures on eBay showed stick figures superimposed over a normal picture that the camera was seeing. If this worked as it appeared in the listing, then this would be a far better and easier device to use. It did look from the advert that maybe the reversed picture was still an issue, possibly confirming what the previous company had told me. This SLS camera was made using a second-hand tablet computer, and inevitably a second-hand Microsoft Xbox 360 SLS camera sensor, so the whole cost was comparatively reasonable. I ordered one and waited for it to come.

Although ordered at different times, both the American SLS camera and the Ovilus 3 arrived at our house in the same delivery on the same day. I turned them both on, and tried them out in the house, just to make sure I understood how to use them. Sure enough, as suspected, the SLS camera did have a reversed image on screen, but the picture quality was excellent. I took the Ovilus out into the garden at night, to see if I could get Roger to try and use it. I had it on for 10 minutes, and just one word came through – "difficult". I'm sure this was Roger trying to use it, and *difficult* was a totally appropriate word for him to use, as I'm sure it is difficult for a spirit to use. I am convinced it must take practice by the spirit in order to be able to use it, but for a first attempt, I give Roger 10 out of 10! Even with practice, I suspect the Ovilus still might not be easy to use.

Although I have read how the Ovilus works, and in some ways it sounds simple, I still can't really understand how the spirit operates it, and also I can't understand how the inventor came up with the concept in the first place. Apparently, it detects the change in the EMF field, air pressure, and temperature, then allocates each of 2240 words a different EMF level, which is 1/2240th of the overall EMF level – no, I don't understand that either!

I did actually message Bill Chapell at Digital Dowsing with a couple of particular questions about the Ovilus, and surprisingly, he did reply very quickly. It was over Christmas, and maybe he was at a loose end, being a boffin, but whatever the reason, I was very grateful for his replies. I did ask him how he came up with the concept, but he didn't respond to that; he said he "doesn't do chat". I suppose that's a typical boffin's reply.

The technical question that I asked him was whether the Ovilus would work in a room that had high background levels of EMF, which our living room sometimes does, for some reason unknown to me. He explained that the Ovilus works on *changes* in EMF, so it will work in high levels of background EMF. I did try it in the living room after this, and sure enough, it did seem to work just as well. One thing he told me was not to have different items of electronic equipment too close together. He suggested the Ovilus shouldn't be within 6 inches of another device, as he had seen in a video I sent him of Roger on camera, where he noticed my Ovilus was next to the EMF meter. I have found that although the EMF meter will flash each time the Ovilus announces a word, I can tell that the EMF meter is being triggered by the Ovilus, so I'm not fooled into thinking it's a spirit each time triggering the EMF meter. When a spirit (Roger) does trigger the EMF meter, it is a random flash of the K2 lights, not simultaneous with any other device doing something specific at that moment. The problem for me is that I need all the equipment within view of the iPhone, so that I've got a permanent record of all the video I'm taking.

The next day Caroline was at work, so I decided I would try the SLS camera and the Ovilus at the cemetery to see if anything might happen. My hopes weren't high – I really didn't expect to see anything on the SLS camera. I thought this would be a very long, maybe impossible, marathon, trying to get any sight of Roger on camera. So, once I arrived at the cemetery, with Poppy our elderly and infirm spaniel in her pushchair, I got to the grave. I got Poppy out and let her potter around while I turned the equipment on. As soon as the SLS camera was running, and I tried talking to Roger, I just couldn't believe what I was seeing – Roger was actually there on camera!

The camera worked exceptionally well, but with the image being reversed, as the English SLS camera manufacturer had told me it would be, as with all these Xbox 360 SLS cameras. It did make it harder than ideal to comprehend where things actually were. I had a long session with Roger, more than 20 minutes, and Roger was there almost all of that time – it was *me* who told *him* I would have to leave, something I felt slightly guilty about. He talked using the Ovilus and flashed the EMF meter. It was absolutely amazing, but I realised that the reversed picture really was a nuisance, and even though it worked a hundred times better than the English SLS camera had ever worked, having a normal picture with stick figures superimposed onto that picture, it still was very awkward, trying to instantly work out where the stick figure was, relative to the gravestones.

I did message the American SLS camera manufacturers about the reversed picture, to ask them if there was any way it could be corrected, whatever the cost. I would have paid almost any price to get it the right way round, as I could see just how good it was, even with the reversed picture. I didn't get any replies initially, but then Caroline noticed that their replies had ended up in my spam box. Once I started talking to them, they were then away for a few weeks on holiday, so I didn't get very far. I never did get an answer from them about rectifying the reversed picture, so I realised I would have to find the solution myself.

Reading up on the internet about reversing pictures, I thought that if I upgraded the tablet computer to a better model which could run Windows 10 software, this better software would enable the picture to be reversed, making the SLS picture display the right way round. The tablet I had only had Windows 7 and couldn't take Windows 10. Windows 10 apparently had a *mirror* function, which I thought would do the job. Also, reading about the Microsoft Kinect software that this SLS camera used, I read that a faster computer, with bigger memory than the Toshiba tablet had, would allow the software to run better – the Kinect software uses a massive amount of computing power and memory to run it, and even the best spec' tablet computers weren't as high a spec' as the software ideally required for optimum performance.

I tried two or three different tablet computers, but for various reasons none of them worked properly. I thought a Microsoft Surface Pro would be my ultimate tablet computer, although lots of reviews said it was incredibly unreliable, and had terrible battery problems. The one I got certainly proved these reviews correct! A few times it flattened its battery for no obvious reason. It got incredibly hot, which made the software keep crashing, and in the end, in trying to sort it out, the tablet effectively destroyed itself. I'd had a very expensive few weeks! Even though these devices weren't new, this whole mini-adventure still cost hundreds of pounds, and I was no nearer to sorting the reversed-picture problem out.

I did finally get a virtually new tablet computer, a Geo, which so far, fingers crossed, has been excellent. It runs the software reliably, and has excellent battery life and doesn't get hot. In theory, the processor speed is similar to the little Toshiba tablet, but it does have a lot more memory, and in side-by-side trials that I've done, the SLS camera software does allow a stick figure to stay on the physical human being more accurately when the person in the picture moves – it just tracks any movement a lot better. That is the only difference I can see in the way the two devices cope with the Microsoft Kinect software. The big benefit of this Geo tablet is that it has a number of extra ports on it, whereas the Toshiba only had one mini-USB. Having extra ports allows me to have a monitor which the tablet computer runs, and this monitor has a *mirror flip* function, which sorts out the problem of the reversed picture. I had found that Windows 10 can't display the picture the right way round after all. The *mirror* function in Windows 10 merely allows extra monitors to be run, over and above the main computer display. It seems I have misunderstood what the word *mirror* actually means! I have looked into other ways, and other devices, to sort the picture out, but the monitor I ended up with has been excellent. The monitor runs off my rechargeable 12-volt lithium-ion battery, which now runs the SLS camera. Initially, as supplied, the SLS ran on disposable batteries, but they didn't last long at all, so I replaced that setup with an excellent rechargeable battery. The tablet computer has its own inbuilt battery, which has a very long life. In experiments, I have found that the whole setup will run for more than two hours before the lithium-ion battery for the camera and monitor goes flat first. This is more than enough for what I need, although I have used most of that running time on occasion, particularly when I filmed at a Stephen Holbrook show – read about it in a later chapter.

Although having an extra screen, of course, adds some weight to the whole setup, I find that the weight is acceptable.

I have mounted the tablet computer low down in the original C frame that I got initially with the SLS camera, and the monitor is mounted on an adjustable computer bracket, which is on top of the C-frame, the battery being at the very bottom of the C-frame.

I find the C-frame very convenient to hold in one hand, while I hold my iPhone, Ovilus and K2 meter in the other hand. These are mounted together on a small mobile phone bracket, with flexible tripod legs holding the Ovilus and K2 by means of a Velcro strap, with the Ovilus and K2 visible in the bottom of the iPhone screen. This also allows me to film other things as they might crop up, apart from the monitor screen, as I merely have to move my hand to alter what the iPhone is filming.

The weight of all the devices can become an issue after a few minutes, so I often film things while sitting down, taking the weight of the SLS rig on my legs, or on a tabletop. Caroline did suggest that I might need a special counterbalance arm to hold the SLS camera rig. Many months ago, I did get one which was very sophisticated and it had the spring counterbalanced arm system mounted on a body-worn harness. It did work very well, but I actually haven't really used it, because using it seems to be more hassle than it's worth, and I am nearly always in a fixed position while filming, even if I do move the camera around slightly to view different parts of the room I'm in (like when I filmed Stephen Holbrook, who paces backwards and forwards, and side to side, throughout his show).

On the whole, the SLS camera setup is very reliable, but I have had a couple of issues over the months. Back in the summer last year, the SLS camera suddenly stopped working altogether. I realised that the Xbox 360 SLS camera was the culprit – it had packed up. I bought another unit off eBay, thinking I would be able to use some components out of my replacement unit to mend the first unit. I planned to do this because the original device from America had been modified with a special output lead on it, which I thought was essential for it to operate in the way it was being used. When I opened up the faulty unit, I found that the innards were totally different from the replacement one I had bought, even though the outsides looked identical. Because the replacement one was a brand-new (but obsolete), unused unit in a sealed box, I decided to try using it as it was, with its different lead to my original one. When I plugged it in, I found it worked perfectly. I realised the original one had had its lead replaced in order to get rid of the original very long lead these devices come with. One big benefit of the original long lead is that it has a full-size USB plug on the end, whereas my original one had a mini-USB plug, to suit the original Toshiba tablet. The mini-USB plug had got slightly damaged while I was using it, so it was great to know that this replacement unit was brand-new in every respect. I expected it to be totally reliable, due to the fact it had never been used before I got it.

A few months later my SLS camera did stop working again, which was a huge surprise, as I was halfway through a chat with Roger while on camera. Suddenly he stopped showing up on screen, although I did suspect he was still there. I just couldn't get him to show up again. It was incredibly annoying, as I was in the middle of an important chat with him regarding the latest news to do with this book, and other issues. All chats with Roger are important, of course – how many people get to chat to their deceased relative, while they're there for you to see, on camera?

I assumed that this Xbox 360 SLS camera had also packed up like the first one had. I ordered another unused, unopened unit, just as before, and when it came, I fully expected it to work soon as I plugged it in, but it didn't. I had just the same problems as the first one and I couldn't work out what was going on. Maybe the software on the tablet computer had failed. Or maybe the USB socket in the tablet had failed, but I wasn't sure if this was a likely explanation. I thought I had ruled everything else out,

I was getting desperate, so I asked Caroline to help me with the software, as she is far better at these things than I am.

When she started looking, she found that the USB socket had stopped working, according to the software on the tablet. Sorting this out merely required the computer to be restarted, something I had never realised could be a solution. After the restart, everything was fine, so the Xbox 360 camera that I had installed a few months ago was still working perfectly after all. What a relief! Now I had a spare boxed unit, which hopefully would be insurance against any future failure of the Xbox 360 unit.

I am still using the SLS camera on average once a week to talk to Roger, and sometimes Joan, on camera, and as always, I save the video for future reference. So far, I have more than 100 videos that I've taken of Roger. I'm just so relieved that I had the foresight at the very beginning to film every time I used the SLS camera, as otherwise there would be some really pivotal moments that I would not have got a record of.

If any readers are wanting to try and do something similar, to film a deceased relative or friend, then the way I have done it could hopefully work for you. It definitely does require a spirit who is desperately keen to get their message across. I'm not sure if most discarnate people will be as forthcoming as Roger, but certainly, regarding the equipment, then everything I have found out could work just as well as anything. There is, however, a very large selection of ghost hunting equipment, so maybe something else might suit you better. Trust your instincts and try whatever you suspect could suit you and your loved one. Whatever you do, it will require patience and dedication, but the rewards will be priceless, if and when it works.

Certainly, Roger has proved beyond any doubt whatsoever that these Xbox 360 SLS cameras do see spirits. It's only the sceptics who say these cameras can't see spirits, that it's really a glitch of the camera, and gullible people like me who think it is a spirit. The sceptics will never believe, however much proof they are shown. That is their loss, and their right to believe that. I'm not trying to convince them, as I will never be able to, so entrenched is their refusal to even consider it's possible. But to the undecided out there, of whom there must be millions, Roger's and my evidence might just sway them. Until Joan gave us her amazing signs, and then Roger took things to an even higher level, I would probably have remained sceptical that all this was possible.

In a later chapter on the Society for Psychical Research, you can read how it was proven that this SLS camera really and unequivocally is seeing a spirit, and in my case, I know that spirit is Roger.

The video for this chapter is accessible, as they all are, via the QR code on the cover of this book. In the first part of the video, I talk through what each piece of equipment does, how it can be used. I do mention other equipment that we tried with Roger, but the other devices didn't work for him – maybe he couldn't activate them. I have come to the conclusion that some devices suit certain spirits, while other spirits might get results with other devices. As in physical life here on Earth, some of us like one thing, others might prefer something else.

I did try a Spirit Box, which is basically a small transistor radio which scans rapidly through all the different radio frequencies, and somehow spirits can actually say audible words using the white noise of an untuned radio frequency. I've seen these working on TV programmes, apparently, but Roger couldn't operate it, or, at least, I couldn't hear him operating it.

Another device I tried was a simple voice recorder (dictation machine). I've seen these on TV working well, capturing EVPs (electronic voice phenomena), whereby a spirit can actually talk, audibly, and record their voice. Some people have heard the spirit talk with their own ears, directly – in fact Caroline heard an invisible man talking just the other day in our kitchen – the first time she has experienced this, but who it was, she doesn't know.

Roger couldn't talk into this recorder, or at least, we couldn't hear it. I have asked him to talk directly into the phone while doing a video recording, as this ought to be just the same process, but, again, he hasn't.

The final device I tried with Roger, to no effect, was a new Ovilus 5 device, a later descendant of the Ovilus 3. When I saw these were being made at the beginning of this year, I thought I'd get one to try, and if it worked, I'd sell the Ovilus 3 and recoup some money. This plan didn't work – Roger couldn't seem to operate it like he can the Ovilus 3. All Ovilus models use the same word database, and I assumed that as they work on the same principles, he would operate the later model just as easily as the older one – this definitely wasn't the case. Eventually I sold the Ovilus 5, just happy to know that the Ovilus 3 is Roger's forte, so why change a winning formula?

If you, the reader, want to try a similar hunt to track down your loved one, then hopefully you can get a flavour of what we have tried and found out. I'm certain that in our case it is Joan's, and then Roger's, determination and persistence, which has enabled us to see and communicate with them. As in all these things, the more success you have, the more you want. Even on Roger's best days, he is only able to say a handful of very relevant words on the Ovilus. Also, those relevant words aren't always quite the word you might expect – they can be a bit cryptic, which often seems to be the case with spirits on the ghost hunting TV programmes.

It's because of this that we have engaged the help of some very helpful and gifted mediums, in the hope of getting more comprehensive answers from Roger, which we have successfully done. In other chapters in this book, I describe in detail what the mediums have achieved for us, and how Roger and sometimes Joan, have been so obviously keen to help us in this quest. Many people believe that mediums are indeed able to communicate with the spirits of loved ones – Stephen Holbrook proved that to us with a message from Roger just three weeks after he died – a stunningly accurate message. This was 6 months prior to us embarking on the hunt for Roger using technology.

With the technology we have got, which has been so overwhelmingly successful, we can now hear amazingly accurate messages from mediums, whilst seeing Roger's, and sometimes Joan's, spirit on camera as the message is relayed to us by the medium. I find this all the more fascinating when it is a medium who's almost on the other side of the world (US), while Roger's and Joan's spirits are with us in our living room! It might be that the spirit is simultaneously in the US and here in England – I know spirits can simultaneously be in more than one place. Or, maybe they are just with us in England, and physical distance from the medium to the spirit is not an issue in their communications – I've read this is also the case.

Whatever the explanation, the whole thing is utterly breathtaking, which is why Joan and Roger are making their story available to us all, so we can learn from what they have both recently learnt.

So, back to the video for this chapter – the latter part, after describing each individual device, is a video which Caroline took of me operating all the equipment in the way I normally use it. This turned out to be so instructive – I know Roger had planned this down to the very last detail. As I turn on the equipment, when I get the SLS camera software operating on the tablet computer, Roger is there immediately on camera. He is there instantly whenever there is a compelling reason for him to be there, otherwise he can take a while to show up. There could be times when circumstances beyond his control cause him to be slow to show up, but in this video, he was definitely keen to show you the viewer how he does it. I hope you are as impressed as I am with what Roger is doing.

I knew these SLS cameras worked, are able to see spirits, but I have never seen any spirit do what Roger has done – continue to show up every time the camera is turned on, over a long period of time (two years so far, as this book goes to the printers). He shows up for as long as an hour on camera if the occasion demands.

The footage I've seen on TV programmes has normally been a short, fleeting appearance of a spirit, just a matter of seconds. I have seen one or two programmes where the ghost hunter has identified the spirit as a relative of the homeowner, but the ones I've seen, it's been someone who the living relative wasn't familiar with, maybe a relative from a couple of generations ago. I haven't seen an ongoing, regular meeting of a deceased family member with a living family member.

Even if it has been done before, (I haven't seen it), that doesn't diminish my astonishment that Joan and Roger would bother to get our attention in order to encourage and guide us to track them down in the afterlife, *on camera*.

It is the visual proof of the afterlife on camera which is the total game-changer for me. Like probably most human beings, for me, seeing is believing. Seeing Joan and Roger, alive and well in the afterlife (which is all around us, in our living rooms and everywhere we physically inhabit) is the one lesson from them that is taking a lot of adjusting to. After a lifetime of not believing in my early Catholic religion (although I did still believe in some sort of God, and I believed in all the Christian values to live by, for instance, treating others as you would want to be treated yourself), I am now having to reassess everything I thought I knew, and everything I believed in, or didn't believe in. I had thought religion was a ridiculously far-fetched concept, pretty bonkers really, but Joan's and Roger's proof on camera that the afterlife is real has knocked me for six, in a positive way.

The biggest irony of all is that Roger didn't believe in life after death, but I think this is the very reason why he has bent over backwards to get his message through to us – that he was wrong. What a pleasant surprise he must have had, the day his body died, to find out that he hadn't disappeared into an eternal blackhole. What a beautiful surprise for him to find that the human story really isn't life and death, as many think, but more accurately, life incarnate and life discarnate. And the most miraculous part of Roger's story, after being instigated by Joan, is that both of them are sharing their astounding story with us, and we are sharing their story with you, the readers and viewers of this phenomenal story. What an honour for us all, to listen to and to learn from their truly inspirational and revelatory first-hand experiences!

There are some very big lessons here for all of us. Some very big readjustments to our beliefs, for many of us. Later in the book, we will review those big lessons we need to digest, but for now, just remember, technology really can help you to communicate with and see your loved one after their physical body dies. Don't believe the sceptics who say this is all rubbish. We know it's not, and you could find out first-hand too that it genuinely is real. You wouldn't be reading this book in the first place if you weren't very curious and inquisitive, as we were, and still are, so I would urge you to give it a go. Try using technology to contact your loved one – you just might be totally amazed with what, and who, you find. Good luck!

Stop Press!

I've already described how Roger's book doesn't follow convention. Within days of having to commit this book to the publishers in its final version, he comes out with yet more fantastic evidence at an Undertaker's Chapel in Yorkshire. The Undertaker has been so enthusiastic in allowing us to film with the SLS camera within his Chapel of Rest. I first met the Undertaker at a Stephen Holbrook show, where he was seeing Stephen to ascertain whether there was anything in this whole *medium* business. He is open minded, willing to be persuaded. He has had some experiences within the mortuary, which he now concedes could be spirits – he has felt someone gently touch him on his left shoulder while he is preparing someone for their funeral. This has happened to him several times. He realises this could be the spirit of the person he's attending to. It stands to reason that a spirit would be watching what's being done to their own body, prior to their funeral. Many mediums agree that spirits almost always attend their own funeral – presumably seeing how well their family are organising the event, and if there's a decent turnout!

Two years after Roger first showed up on the SLS camera, he's still doing it! A couple of weeks ago I fortuitously got in touch with an American physicist with an amazingly impressive CV, who also happens to be a paranormal investigator. Mark Wentz has had many paranormal experiences of his own, too many and varied to detail here. The bit that is so helpful for this book, is that he uses an SLS camera himself, and has filmed his mum's spirit on the camera in the manner of me filming Joan and Roger.

Here's Mark's explanation of how the camera works:

> Jeremy, after reading your description on how the SLS camera works, it seems to me you already have a good handle on how it works. As I said in an earlier email, my understanding of how it works is that the system sends out a grid pattern of infrared waves, similar to the way a radar sends out radio or microwave waves. The sensor then detects the infrared waves that reflect back to the system. The Kinetic X software then analyses those signals looking for straight lines that join and move together. These lines, in the original design and use for a Wii game, are the appendages of a human playing the game. The software design built into the Kinetics X is,

> as you have pointed out in your book is quite elaborate and does require some significant computing power to work properly. I believe the reason the stick figures sometimes flicker in and out is because the software is having a hard time finding the straight-line configuration in the reflected wave pattern and takes time to do the computations needed to show the stick figure. The software looks for human type shapes. So, what reflects back the infrared waves depends on the shape, motion and material composition of the objects within range of the transmitting device. It is my experience working with spirits that they indeed can manipulate electrical and electromagnetic energies. I believe that is what they are doing to present themselves with all electronic systems, the SLS system in particular. Are you familiar with the Scole Experiments? I will get back with you asap. Take Care

The video of Joan and Roger in the funeral home is accessible with all the other videos for this book, titled Chapter 3, Equipment Used – Bonus Video. Also, do investigate the **Scole Experiments** (on YouTube) if you're not familiar with them – you'll be absolutely dumbfounded with what occurs!

In the video you will see Joan's and Roger's spirits, waiting patiently in the Chapel of Rest while I film them. I had asked Roger a few days prior to the filming to join us if he could, as I was fascinated to see who might show up. As far as I can tell, only Joan and Roger show up, no other spirits, which tends to reinforce in my mind that Joan and Roger only show up because they choose to – they manipulate the electronic technology to make us see them.

Recently Roger has made me realise this is how it works – a couple of times he has said *coarse* on the Ovilus, when I ask him if this is how he shows to us, which I take to mean *of course* (there is no word *course* in the Ovilus database). He is using the word *coarse* like the word *yes,* which he has never used.

I have edited out the Undertaker's name, so there are a couple of points where the video is slightly jumpy. The whole length of video taken at the Undertakers was 20 minutes and Joan and Roger were showing up for around 17 minutes of that time – that shows you how keen they are to help us with our investigations!

Chapter 4

Joan and Roger's Grave

In around 2015, Roger got Caroline and me to go round to his house to hear what he had planned when he and Joan eventually died. At this meeting there was a Humanist celebrant, who described to us what was entailed with a Humanist service, which is what Roger had planned for them both. Even though Joan and Roger had been religious in their earlier years, Roger was now of the opinion that religion wasn't something he believed in anymore. Whether Joan was of this opinion too, I'm not sure, but whatever Roger decided, Joan went along with willingly.

When Joan died just before Christmas 2017, it was very sudden, without warning, at home, and it took us all by surprise. I had always felt that Roger would probably die first, and I'm certain that's what he thought too. Once Joan died, there was a lot to organise, as there always is when anyone dies. This kept everyone busy, doing all the routine paperwork, fetching certificates, liaising with the undertakers, etc. It is this enforced busyness that keeps people occupied and slightly relieves the pressure of such a momentous event. Caroline and I did everything we could to help Roger, as of course did Alison and Colin. Between the five of us, we kept each other's spirits up as much as possible and supported each other through this sudden turn of events.

One of the things that Roger did by himself was to organise Joan's headstone for her grave. Roger had, some years ago, bought two adjoining plots in the local cemetery where Joan was to be buried, with Roger joining her sometime in the future. The headstone was to commemorate Joan, with space left for Roger's details when the time came.

The stone Roger ordered was a simple black granite headstone with minimal wording. Both Alison and Caroline felt it was too plain, but it was their dad's choice, so didn't try to persuade him to have something slightly wordier or fancier; they respected his decision, as Roger had said they both liked plain headstones such as the type you see in military cemeteries.

Caroline found everything to do with her mother's death painfully hard to come to terms with, or even to talk about. Initially she visited the grave only occasionally, but always very reluctantly.

In February 2020, Roger suddenly decided that Joan's headstone was too plain. He sought Caroline and Alison's advice about what do with the headstone, whether to get it redone, and if so, what the wording should be. This apparently sudden change of mind by Roger was a surprise to us all, especially when Roger asked why no one had said anything before about it being too plain. We all assured him that because he had seemed so certain about what he wanted from the beginning, it wasn't anyone else's business to suggest something different.

Caroline took it upon herself to investigate and talk to the headstone company, to see what was possible. It became apparent that to get the face of the existing headstone redone would be virtually the same price as to get a whole new headstone made from scratch, even with the cost of getting the old headstone disposed of. The company that made the headstone initially said it would take between four to six months to get it remade, so Caroline decided to go to another company who said they could do it within a matter of weeks, and they would be cheaper, to boot.

Once the ball was rolling, Caroline and I visited various local cemeteries under the guise of walking the dog to investigate what other people had on their headstones, what sort of writing was used, what wording, etc. It was very illuminating, and a good education in the art of what constitutes a good headstone.

We took many photographs and reported back to Roger and Alison about what looked appropriate, and what didn't.

New wording was decided by Roger, Caroline and Alison, with Roger going with what Caroline and Alison suggested. Within a few weeks the design was finalised. All of this took place during the height of the COVID-19 pandemic when ordinary day-to-day life was suspended, and everyone in this country lived surreal lives, living by an alien set of rules.

The new headstone arrived in the middle of July, some weeks later than initially expected due to COVID-19. It was still reasonably quick, all things considered. Everyone was happy with the new headstone, and I'm sure Roger was relieved to have eventually given Joan the fitting monument to her life that she deserved.

The old headstone was delivered to our house, where we installed it in our garden as part of a collection of things to commemorate Joan and other past family members.

Roger died just less than two years later. Caroline and I resumed our dog walking mission in cemeteries, to investigate how to implement the final version of the grave once Roger and Joan were lying together forever. Joan's grave was purely a headstone in a grassy field, amongst others. Many people had created attractive and fitting graves to their own personal liking, so it was inevitable that Roger and Joan would have a grave that was in keeping, and appropriate to the people that they were whilst in the physical world.

In our local cemetery there were many impressive graves from as early as the 1800s, and in those days, families would spare no expense to create beautiful memorials to the loved ones they had lost. At that time, it was common to have the grave surrounded by a low cast-iron fence, often moderately ornate, but always very impressive. The belief was that an iron fence would keep the spirits in, both within the grave, and also within the graveyard. Hence graveyards would have iron fences all around, with iron gates as well.

One idea that Caroline and I liked was to have a picture of her mum and dad on the back of the headstone, as we saw a number of modern gravestones which had pictures on. They can be very attractive, and tend to personalise the grave, which otherwise can look a bit too formal. Alison was not keen on this idea, thinking it would not be appropriate.

We did continue to investigate the idea of a picture. Because the back of the gravestone faces the footpath, people tend to approach the grave from the back. Initially it seemed like a golden opportunity to do something on the back of the gravestone, as otherwise it could look as if a great opportunity had been missed. Once this headstone was done there would be no changes to be made in the future, so it demanded a lot of thought before every possible idea was literally set in stone.

Eventually, Alison did agree to the picture as she said that she wouldn't visit the grave very often, and as Caroline and I had become graveyard connoisseurs, if that's what we wanted, then she was happy for that to be done. We were very pleased with her generous change of heart – we knew she wouldn't regret it.

We continued to work out all the details for this grave – luckily, we had six months to get everything organised before the headstone could be installed in its final position. This was purely due to Council regulations, that headstones had to be installed no sooner than six months after a burial. This gave us all plenty of time to think long and hard about what would be right, what Joan and Roger would want and be happy with.

The idea of cast-iron fencing was considered, and many ways of doing it were looked at, from reusing old cast-iron panels of various types, such as cast-iron grills used in floors in churches and greenhouses over heating pipes, to modern cast-iron lawn edging. These are panels which are just pushed down into the soil, to give a decorative finished edge between the lawn and the flowerbed. This lawn edging idea seemed favourite, but the available types all seemed a bit too small and puny. Eventually we saw a modern but old-fashioned looking cast-iron lawn edging that was much longer than all the others we'd seen. We got a sample, and this looked perfect for the job. We spoke to the supplier to see if they had enough for our needs, as we would need 12 of these pieces. They checked the stock at their various depots, and found that they had just enough in France, so we bought them all, even though we wouldn't be installing them for several months.

Once the gravestone had the new wording for Roger, the final job was to have the picture put on the back. The company doing it were exceptionally helpful. We visited them several times to talk to them about how they made gravestones, and to see the various processes involved. It was so impressive to see all the skill being used in creating such permanent memorials to loved ones. We saw a white marble headstone for a young girl being hand sculpted to form the wings of an angel around the top and sides of the headstone. The lady who owned the company, who I will call *Angie,* was such a pleasant, friendly and helpful individual.

Angie and her husband were so warm and reassuring. We went over to their premises to see the picture being created on the back of the headstone. It was produced by a process called impact etching, in which a diamond tipped stylus hammers into the surface of the granite, chipping microscopic amounts of the black granite away to leave a slightly rough white surface. The computer-controlled machine would take a couple of hours to create the whole picture.

Talking to Angie and her husband was always a breath of fresh air. We could talk to her totally honestly about anything to do with Joan and Roger, about funerals, about life after death, ghosts, indeed absolutely anything. She always had time for us, even though she was a very busy lady. She and her company always put the customer first, which so many companies don't.

Whatever the customer wanted in terms of memorials, her company would try to achieve. The results speak for themselves.

One incredibly moving headstone her company had created was for a young boy who had died. His whole life was devoted to scooters, the sort with small wheels like little skateboard wheels. His very wide memorial (about 2 metres) was a black granite headstone, into which was carved his scooter and safety helmet, the little details of which were coloured in. It looked like the scooter and helmet were real, but they were solid granite! His smiling face was printed on the granite, along with some heart-breaking wording. His parents obviously loved him way beyond words. The pain some people feel when they lose someone is so utterly overwhelming. What can be worse than losing a child? At least losing an elderly parent is predictable, expected. How can anyone live a normal life after losing their child?

One of the things that we and Angie were in total agreement about was how people should be allowed to commemorate their loved ones with whatever headstone they want and have the whole grave just as they wish. Some cemeteries have a long list of various strict rules, which just seem to have been written to be awkward and vindictive. Apparently church cemeteries are the worst for this. When people are at their lowest ebb, surely they should be allowed to do things in the way that gives them some degree of comfort?

Caroline and I have had a couple of guided walks around cemeteries, which have been fascinating and eye-opening. The most impressive memorial I have ever seen on a grave was in a large cemetery in York – a young man who had had a scrap car business had been buried there, and his memorial was a large white marble, accurately and very intricately carved, old car. It was a replica of an actual American car from the 1920s – the detail was out of this world. The talent of the monumental masons was absolutely off the scale.

The photograph used to create Joan and Roger's artwork was a photograph taken at a previous house that Alison had lived in some years before. It captured them both perfectly in a happy pose for the camera. The artwork on the back of the gravestone was a good size, making the most of the available space. It is a fantastic tribute to Caroline and Alison's parents.

The new stone was installed into position by the monumental masons a few days earlier than we expected. Caroline and I were planning to visit the cemetery to walk Poppy and to measure up where exactly the stone needed positioning. We were going to tell the monumental masons the exact position, as Joan and Roger's graves were very close to the neighbouring graves, so the position of the headstone was crucial. If the position was wrong, even by just one or two inches, the final grave would look distorted once the cast-iron fencing was in place around the border.

As I was getting the dog ready to leave our house to go to the cemetery, I was sitting in the living room on the stool which is very near the fuse box in the house. Suddenly a circuit breaker (resettable fuse), tripped out with a loud bang, as one of the electrical circuits disconnected. It was very bizarre, as nothing particular had caused this as far as I could tell. I reset the circuit breaker, and it did it again within a few seconds. Again, no obvious reason.

We went to the cemetery, and as soon as we arrived, we noticed that the headstone had been placed in the wrong position. It was several inches to one side from where it should have been. The fuse box incident was definitely Roger warning us that the headstone needed checking. He knew it was wrong, and we needed to have a look.

We took measurements and marked out the ground so that the masons would know exactly where the stone should be.

Once we were home Caroline contacted the company and told them what needed to be done. Within a day or two the mistake was rectified.

A few days later we went to the grave with the cast-iron fence panels, plastic anti-weed membrane, a dozen bags of slate chippings, and various tools. We spent a very arduous day preparing the grave, which entailed digging the excess soil and grass away and levelling it. Even though it looked nearly flat when the burial had been completed, the gravediggers left a little mound of soil above Roger's grave. Levelling it was much harder work than I had expected. I'm certainly less fit than I was, with a lot less stamina than I had a few decades ago.

Once levelled, we positioned the plastic membrane over the soil around the gravestone, then gently pushed and hammered in the cast-iron edgings around the perimeter. They went in easily in places, and here and there they were stubborn, but eventually we got them all into position, and they did look excellent. The final job was to place the slate chippings onto the plastic membrane. I thought a dozen bags would be plenty, but actually it wasn't enough, so we returned the following day with another dozen bags to finish the job.

The whole grave looked superb – we were proud to have given Joan and Roger the best looking grave in the cemetery.

On 5 November, a couple of weeks after we had completed the grave, Caroline's sister, Alison, rang, enquiring whether we fancied going to the cemetery after dark that night to let off some fireworks which she had found in Roger's garage whilst clearing out his effects. These rockets were many years old, so we weren't even sure if they would work properly, but as we had a couple of our grandchildren staying with us, we decided we would join them at the cemetery to see what would happen. Both Caroline and I had been reluctant to go to the cemetery in the dark, because we wondered if it would be scary. Even though in the daylight hours the cemetery felt very welcoming and a lovely place to be, we had both wondered privately if at night the atmosphere wouldn't be so relaxing.

We met up just as it had got dark, and as we walked into the cemetery what struck us all was how many of the graves had candles or lanterns illuminated at the graveside. I think they were all solar powered or battery-powered devices, but they all looked beautiful. We were surprised we hadn't thought of it ourselves.

It was a lovely evening with a lot of clear sky, with occasional small clouds, and the rockets were let off one at a time by Colin. The displays were fantastic. We dedicated each rocket in turn to the various family members who are no longer with us. Everyone enjoyed it, especially the two young grandsons.

As usual I filmed events on my phone. On reviewing the footage the next day, I noticed a number of light anomalies. A lot of lights on camera could be explained by the various torches that we had with us, lights on the other graves and the lights of the fireworks. When torchlight is filmed on camera, you do get various reflections within the camera lens which can look strange, but I am used to these from all the filming I have been doing, so I could be sure that some of these anomalies really were anomalous.

Some weeks later, Roger did confirm on camera while I was using the Ovilus, that he was with us at the cemetery when we set off the rockets. He did confirm this using the words *anomalies* and *rockets*.

The day after the firework display at the cemetery, Caroline said she wanted some sort of lighting on her parents' grave, so I set my mind to how to do this, in detail. The solution I came up with was to have a small LED candle effect lantern on the front of the gravestone. On the back I planned to have some LEDs sitting in the ground to illuminate Joan and Roger's picture on the rear of the headstone. All of these would be powered by a rechargeable battery which I would change every week or two so that the lights were on permanently, day and night.

After a bit of experimenting, I came up with the system which we installed a few days later. With a few tweaks, the system worked very well. Initially I thought it might require three little LED spotlights for the picture, but in the event one was sufficient. It was necessary to balance lighting versus battery life, so the one spotlight along with the battery lantern turned out to give a battery life of more than 10 days without a problem. This requires us to go to the cemetery normally every weekend to change the battery and attend to the grave, to remove old leaves which could have covered the spotlight in the ground.

In conversations with Roger, he is very happy with the whole grave and the illuminations.

After the grave was finished, Angie and her husband from the headstone company came to visit the grave. She took some photos to use in the company's sales literature. Caroline was so pleased with what the company had created, she was more than happy to let everyone who was interested see pictures of it. Such a large etched picture was unusual on a headstone – Roger was always keen to lead the way.

Whilst chatting at the graveside, Angie asked me if I had ever read a book, *Journey of Souls*; I had never heard of it. She explained that it is written by a hypnotherapist, Michael Newton, who had hypnotised dozens of his patients over the years and been able to get them to reveal deep-seated memories of previous lives.

When I later read the book, it explained how every patient had memories which were all very similar to other patients' memories: They all tended to prove that when we die, our soul reincarnates some years later, and we live another physical life on Earth.

I was so amazed. I had never heard of this before. I read a number of books on the same subject, and they all corroborated each other. There is a consensus that reincarnation is what we do when we die. We each live about half a dozen lives on Earth, learning various lessons in each lifetime, until we have reached the highest level, at which point we don't come back to Earth again.

Each lifetime cycle is about 140 years long, so if we die at 80, we will be a soul in the afterlife for around 60 years, then will be reborn as another physical person.

I thought Roger's proof of life after death was incredible enough, but this all sounds even more incredible. When I've asked Roger about this, if he knows about reincarnation, he says on the Ovilus that he hasn't heard about it, but in later messages through medium Liz Murphy, Roger says he does know about reincarnation – read about it in Chapter 9.

When I first saw Roger's spirit and came to terms with the fact that there is life after death, that's what he is showing me, after all, I assumed he would have all the answers to my questions – he would know everything there is to know. Subsequent reading of dozens of books has revealed that when we die, we don't suddenly know everything – we continue to learn, even in the afterlife. This is what eternal life is all about – a continual learning process. This is the very reason why we live here on Earth, to learn everything we need to over several lifetimes.

If we don't absorb certain lessons in this lifetime, we will be back on Earth again, relearning that lesson in our next lifetime, until that lesson sticks. This is why some of us have a hard life – it's our opportunity to learn something important, so it sticks in our mind.

Roger's lessons for me were really taking shape. I was beginning to understand everything that proof of the afterlife implies. I will never view life in the same way as I did the day before Roger first appeared to me on the SLS camera. Far from this life being a few years of something, then an eternity of nothing, this life is just a practice run, a short series of lessons to take on board which our soul will remember forever, until our next physical life, when we will do it all over again in another physical body. Our souls tend to meet up in their various physical lifetimes. These soul groups are a recurring theme. Apparently, the soul of our parent could come back in the next lifetime as the soul of our grandchild or great grandchild! How bizarre and far-fetched this all sounds – but apparently it is real, this really is what life is all about.

I, for one, wouldn't have believed any of this, had I not seen Roger's spirit on camera!

Roger's appearances on camera have made me reappraise everything I thought I knew. My supposedly logical brain has had to go right back to the drawing board and start putting my beliefs back together from the starting point that we live forever. Roger and Joan have proved this to me.

Thanks, Joan and Roger, for giving me the lesson of all lessons!

Chapter 5

Poppy, Our Beloved Spaniel

We got Poppy in 2007, during the wettest summer for decades. She was a six-week-old cocker spaniel puppy – a really tiny thing who could fit in the palm of my hand. Within just a few weeks she slept on our bed, and she did that for the rest of her life. There were times when it was a little awkward, being in the bed with her, but as for many dog owners, she very soon became one of the family, probably the most important one. When the children were small, we had a German shepherd, Emma, who was a guard dog, and she looked after the children very, very assiduously. When she died at 11 years of age, I knew I had to have a big say in what type of dog we got next, otherwise Caroline would suddenly come home with a dog that possibly wasn't the ideal dog from my point of view. It was a nice change to have a smaller dog than a German shepherd. It makes it so much easier having a smallish dog for taking them around in the car or picking them up when the occasion demands.

We took her everywhere with us. Whenever we visited people or went away for any reason, even to hotels, Poppy would come with us. The only time we both left her was for 10 days when we went to America to see Caroline's friend. This was a once-in-a-lifetime trip for me, as I had never been to America before, but Caroline had been many times with her job over the years.

Poppy had quite a gentle nature. She was fairly friendly with adults, but not so much with children, who she merely tolerated. A difficult child would make her raise her lip as if she was getting ready to snap at them. Certainly, she wasn't one of those dogs who are friendly to everyone, but Caroline and me, well, she adored us, and we adored her. She was also reasonably friendly with many dogs, but bizarrely she wasn't so keen on other spaniels, especially spaniel puppies, who she hated with a vengeance. Maybe she was just jealous or lacking in self-confidence. She could be a jealous dog. Also, she could sulk for hours or even days over the most trivial of things. Sometimes we wouldn't even know why she was sulking – exactly the same personality trait as some children (not ours, of course!).

The first few years she wasn't that bothered about food, but when my mother came to live with us with her mongrel, Rose, suddenly Poppy loved her food, and Rose's too, if she got the chance, which she often did. Poppy rapidly became top dog – poor Rose was bullied by Poppy, which I was unable to stop her from doing, even though Rose was the bigger dog. I suppose it was partly because Rose moved into Poppy's house, so Rose would inevitably be the underling. Also, Rose's temperament was very laid back, so Poppy took advantage. Another quirk of Poppy's was that she never liked having her photograph taken – somehow, she always knew what was happening, and she would go out of her way to spoil the photograph, or even to not be in the photograph in the first place. Again, just the same personality trait as some children.

When Caroline's mum, Joan, died, Caroline got extremely close to Poppy, closer than she'd ever been previously. She was a very important crutch in Caroline's life, helping her get through the overwhelming grief that she felt. When Caroline and I visited Joan at the undertakers in her coffin, Poppy came with us, and she gave us both some sort of helpful reassurance at this incredibly sad time.

Once Joan had died, Roger made quite a fuss of Poppy, which he had never done previously, and Poppy reciprocated by always being pleased to see Roger, waiting for any little treats such as biscuits or other snacks that he offered her. We were always conscious that Poppy shouldn't eat too much, as she had a tendency to be a bit heavier than she should be, but we couldn't tell Roger to not feed her, so we used to just watch as she tucked into a whole range of snacks when we visited.

Roger didn't seem like much of a dog person, but when Caroline was a teenager, they did have two border collies which Caroline doted on, and Roger was also very keen on.

As Poppy got older, especially once she was into double-figures, she couldn't walk as far as she used to. When we first moved to Goole, she was 11 years old and she could still walk reasonably well, but long distances were getting a bit much, so we would drive to the local park and then let her walk around the park. We did walk to the park, around it and back home, a few times, but it was an ordeal for her, as she had a heart condition.

When COVID-19 hit, Poppy was our excuse for our one bit of daily exercise out of the house, so we used to make the most of it and amble round the local park or other suitable walking areas. We would normally tie it in with a visit to Roger, to see if he needed anything, or just to visit him and have an illegal cup of coffee in his living room, or if the weather wasn't bad, we might have a drink in the garden with him.

During Roger's illnesses in his last year, Poppy was a continuing great comfort to Caroline. When Roger died, Poppy was an even greater comfort for both of us. She gave us the reason to keep living an ordinary daily life. Her affection for us was crucial at this time. We would regularly take Poppy to the cemetery where Joan was buried, while we were upgrading her headstone. But now that Roger had died, we were visiting the cemetery even more often in readiness for Roger's funeral, and we were starting to make plans for Joan and Roger's combined grave.

The day before Roger's funeral, Poppy had a stroke while we were at home. This was a real knockout blow for us, as we thought we were going to have two deaths to deal with in the space of a few days. For several hours we sat with Poppy while she lay virtually unconscious on the settee, and then on the garden bench when we took her outside into the sunshine. We thought we were saying our goodbyes to her. She lay there, not even responding to our attempts at comforting words for her, through floods of tears. I knew that Caroline would be absolutely devastated if Poppy were to die now. Of course, we knew that she was an old dog, she wouldn't go on forever, but surely now wasn't going to be the time for her to die?

After many hours, she actually perked up. Miraculously, she even started walking a little bit before she would collapse on the floor. Over the next few weeks, we got into a routine with her, walking reasonably some days, and not walking at all on other days. We got a dog pushchair to wheel her around in, so she would ride in it while we had a walk, and then if she was up to it, we would get her out to have a short potter around before getting back in her pushchair. At the cemetery, it was like having her own personal park, as no other dogs were there, and no other people generally, so she could totter in complete safety, and just sniff around until it was time to go home.

In February of this year, she developed a cough, which I knew was linked to her heart problem. The vet had said some months before that she was doing as well as she could, so we just had to enjoy our time with her, with whatever she was able to do. Generally, she had been a fairly healthy dog, although around the age of 10, she did have a couple of big operations for cancer, which was a big shock to us at the time, but she got through those with no continuing problems.

One evening after her meal she became very uncomfortable, and we sat up with her throughout the night, either together, or taking it in turns. I was getting worried that we might need to get the vet in the morning, as I didn't want her to suffer more than she had to. She died at about six in the morning, lying on the settee, with Caroline stroking her and comforting her. Unfortunately, I had to go to work at 6:30, and it was something

I couldn't get out of at such short notice. Somehow, I managed to function in my job, and all the school children got safely delivered to their school without me breaking down in front of them.

Caroline sat with Poppy on the settee, and when I returned from work at 9 o'clock in the morning, I got the SLS camera out and filmed to see if Roger was there, which he was. I didn't really want to film, it almost seemed macabre, but I knew I had to do it, as Roger might give us some even more ground-breaking proof of his continuing existence, which would be yet another bit of proof in his amazing story. He didn't disappoint – he was above Poppy on the settee, and he comforted us all. Caroline and I were unable to speak properly, but I managed to summon up the energy to dig a grave for Poppy in the garden, next to an acer tree which had been Roger's, which we had managed to transplant in the middle of the hot summer, and it had survived, so this became the right place for Poppy's grave. This tree was actually the second acer which we had tried to transplant from Roger's garden; the first one having succumbed to the heat. We had another go with a second acer that he had, and this one had survived after weeks of watering it every hour, day and night (on a timer – we didn't get up out of bed every hour!). This was a fitting spot for Poppy to be buried, along with her lifelong favourite toy rabbit, her leather collar, the sheepskin rug she'd had since being a puppy, and a paw-print blanket.

To finish the grave off, we moved a spaniel sculpture which Caroline had bought me some years before, to take up residence under the tree, above Poppy. We also had one of her personalized dog bowls with her name painted on, filled with a flower arrangement, and a solar powered candle-effect lantern which flickers at night when the sun goes down.

A couple of weeks later, a medium told us that Poppy was still "earthbound". I read books on animals' souls, and in one of these, it said that the soul can reincarnate. We decided that we would get another spaniel puppy in a few months, as it would help us to get through the grief; we would feel very empty without a dog to lavish attention on. We hoped Poppy wouldn't be too jealous and would forgive us for replacing her. Caroline kept telling her that she would always be "the Best": Spaniel number two would always be the *second best.* After much searching, Caroline found a suitable breeder who would have a puppy ready to collect mid-August. This tied in well with our summer guests having returned home, leaving us free to concentrate on the new puppy, giving her our full attention.

Unfortunately, Caroline hadn't been able to locate a suitable puppy anywhere in the UK that would be available at the right time, and which hopefully would be the right colour. We were looking for another black working cocker spaniel, but she could only find a puppy that would be born to brown parents. Although it was possible that a black pup might be born, the chances weren't that high.

Because the breeder was such a lovely person, with exactly the right personality and attitude, and because all her brown cocker spaniels had such great temperaments, I knew this was the right family to give us the best puppy. Surprisingly, the mother only had three puppies, two brown females and one mainly white male. We had first choice, having got our names on the list first, and we chose the brown one with a white flash on its chest like Poppy had, and white hind paws. This puppy just happened to be the bossiest of the three, so we knew we might be getting a handful.

Once this plan was in place it became a project of mine to see whether this new puppy would have Poppy's soul; whether Poppy would reincarnate. First of all, I needed to see if I could locate Poppy's soul, which surprisingly, I am convinced I did in various videos with the SLS camera, whilst talking to Roger's spirit in our living room. As usual, I asked Roger if it was possible for Poppy's soul to reincarnate into the puppy.

Using the Ovilus, Roger did say he wasn't sure, but he did acknowledge Poppy using the words, *poppa, dog, wolf*.

Two weeks after Poppy died, I was filming Roger's spirit in our living room, talking to him, when I saw a second spirit in front of our standard lamp, which is next to the place where Caroline normally sits on the settee. Roger did acknowledge, as before, with the word *poppa*. If this was Poppy's spirit, then this would be the first time I had seen it. This spirit was slightly human-shaped, but smaller than Roger's spirit normally appears. Sceptics would say, if asked, that this couldn't be Poppy's spirit. Sceptics would say that this SLS camera doesn't really see spirits at all; it's merely a glitch of the camera, but I know that it really does see them. A couple of days later I had the chance to try some experiments with a living and breathing physical dog in our living room, when Caroline's sister's dog came to stay with us for a few days.

My first experiment was to see whether the SLS camera would put a stick figure on a dog. However much I tried, the camera wouldn't see Peggy as something to superimpose a stick figure onto. The camera is always looking for human shapes, so anything that it doesn't think is human-shaped doesn't get a stick figure on it. While Peggy was in the living room, I continued to film with the SLS, and Roger continued to acknowledge things on the Ovilus, with the words, *meet, dog, tickle*. At one point, Peggy is looking in the direction of the front door, when very briefly, a little stick figure appears near her, moving past her, and she appears to be following it with her gaze. I am convinced that Peggy could see Poppy's spirit in the room, which just became visible to the SLS camera for a second.

Sceptics will wonder why an animal spirit would show on camera as a human-shaped entity. The reason for this is that the software within the camera is always looking for human shapes, so even though a living dog won't show up with a stick figure on it, if there is a spirit present, the camera can detect that there is something there. As a spirit is basically an amorphous mass of energy, in struggling to make sense of it, the camera, knowing that there is something in its view, does indeed superimpose a human-shaped stick figure onto this cloud-like mass of energy. It is the infrared dots that the camera emits that are being displaced fractionally by the charged air in the vicinity of the spirit, the camera detects this displacement of the million infrared dots it emits, and then struggles to work out what are the features of this spirit. In struggling to make sense of it, the camera will tend to see certain features in the room behind where the spirit is, for instance the shape of the standard lamp, and it will think that the various hard points of the standard lamp are where the features of this spirit are (limbs, torso, head etc.). This is why quite often the spirit on camera can be linked to the features within the room. A good analogy might be to imagine you are walking in thick fog through the local park. You gradually catch up with another person walking in the same direction. Initially, you can just make out that there is someone in the fog, but you're not sure whether it is an adult or child, male or female. Your mind is struggling to interpret who or what it is. With such scant and indistinct visual information, you might initially jump to the wrong conclusion, until you get closer, then suddenly you see who it is – there is no doubt now.

Well, the SLS has exactly the same struggle as you in the fog – minimal information, very ill-defined, but it does know there is someone there, so it makes a best guess based on a vague vision of something, and it puts a stick figure onto its best guess, which might well include the hard features it can see properly, which are the hard features within its vision such as lampshades, furniture, etc.

A week later when I filmed Roger in the living room again, there was the same little stick figure in front of the standard lamp. Over the next few months, every time I filmed Roger in the living room, who would often be in front of the green chair,

I would see a little spirit in front of the standard lamp, who I am convinced was Poppy.

My experiment to see if Poppy would reincarnate into the new puppy was based on the idea that if Poppy's spirit did indeed reincarnate, then the spirit who I took to be Poppy in front of the standard lamp, would at some point stop showing up. This was my theory, and I was keen to see how it turned out when we did eventually get our new puppy.

Once the puppy was born, I would regularly film Roger in the living room, and the little spirit of Poppy was still visible in front of the standard lamp. From what I had read, the soul might not reincarnate straightaway, but quite often it would happen when the puppy was a few weeks old, particularly once its eyes had opened. I was amazed to see that when the new puppy was two or three weeks old, the spirit of Poppy in front of the standard lamp did indeed stop showing on the SLS camera. I couldn't believe what I was seeing, or to be more accurate, not seeing. To me this confirmed that Poppy had indeed reincarnated into Edie, our new puppy.

We collected Edie when she was 10 weeks old in the middle of August as planned. Although her character isn't exactly the same as Poppy's, I did wonder whether or not the character of Poppy could still be there in the new dog. I reread my book about animal souls, to remind myself exactly what the animal medium said. She says that the new animal will not be a clone of the previous one but will actually be a blend of the old soul together with a new soul that the new creature had to start with. This tends to confirm even more strongly that Poppy has reincarnated into Edie, and further filming with the SLS camera when Roger is around tends to confirm to me that this really is the case.

Edie is becoming a lovely dog, but we had forgotten just how lively puppies are. I think Edie is a more energetic dog than Poppy ever was, but she is settling down nicely to fit in with our way of life, and she is certainly giving us all the exercise and love for life that I wanted her to give us. She is helping us to get over the grief of losing Poppy. Of course, we will never forget Poppy, and Caroline still tells Poppy that she will always be *the best*, so Edie will only ever be *second best*. Poor Edie, only ever going to be second best, and the wrong colour as well! Caroline initially was always against having a brown spaniel, with its brown nose. Her ideal had always been a black spaniel with a black nose. I think really that Caroline did believe me when I told her that this new dog would not be a Poppy clone, even if it did have her soul – it would always be a spaniel in its own right, whatever the colour. A good temperament was always the priority, and I was totally confident that Edie would have that. I still struggle to look at pictures or videos of Poppy, it makes me so sad, but the thought that Poppy's soul is happy, and she is still around us in spirit is such a lovely, comforting thought, whether that spirit is in the new puppy, or not.

It is a very strange thing, how proof of eternal life doesn't stop you being sad when a physical being dies. In theory, knowing that life goes on without the physical body means that we should not be devastated when the physical body expires. Many of the books I have read, written by mediums, say that even with this knowledge mediums still suffer the same grief as everyone else when a loved one dies. I suppose we in the West have this culture, that we don't really embrace the afterlife. We talk about it, some go to church on a Sunday, but we don't really believe in it and all its many implications. Roger has proven to us that it's real, but our thinking, our instinctive thoughts, still haven't caught up with the reality that life does indeed go on. It's such a big concept; it really does take a lot of coming to terms with.

The video for this chapter shows the SLS camera footage I filmed of Roger above Poppy's body. Also in the video is a still photo of Roger and Poppy together – this is the only photo of the two of them together that I can find. It was taken in 2018, the year after Joan died. Poppy is holding her ball, which she nearly always did, often while she slept. The arm of the person next to Roger is that of his sister-in-law, but as this chapter is about Poppy (and Roger), I have taken the liberty of cropping her out of the shot (sorry, Barbara – I had to do it).

The first few minutes shows Poppy's body lying on the sofa where she died a couple of hours previously. Roger's spirit appears above her. Note how most of the words Roger says on the Ovilus are exactly the right word: *Letter*, when Roger tells us that a letter has just been delivered by the postman; *difficult*, which at the time I took to mean that the situation is difficult for us to come to terms with, but possibly Roger is talking about the difficulty with trying to get the SLS camera to work in the way I want – I was trying to get the picture the right way round, as they normally display a mirror image of what they are looking at. I am telling Roger that if a new lead comes from Amazon today, if it works, then finally it will allow me to display the computer image on a monitor, which will allow me to display the image un-mirrored, therefore the correct way round (the monitor has this facility inbuilt). This subsequently did happen successfully.

Either way, whatever Roger meant, it is definitely Roger's intelligence in our living room, his mind as sharp as it ever was, even though he has no physical body (or physical brain). How would a super-sceptic explain this? Is this stick figure on the SLS camera a *glitch* or a *bug*? Of course it isn't. It's Roger's spirit, no question about it.

The second half of the video for this chapter is a video taken three weeks after Poppy died, when we had Caroline's sister's dog, Peggy, to stay. I had tried to see if the SLS camera would put a stick figure onto a living dog, but it never did. I had already noticed this when Poppy was alive, but I was just double checking. There are some brief glimpses of a little stick figure above Caroline's head, in front of the standard lamp (this is illuminated, so it's hard to see any detail of the lampshade). When I look at Peggy in her dog bed on the floor, I am asking if Poppy is there. Roger gives a number of excellent clues on the Ovilus. This part of the video doesn't show the Ovilus, as I have zoomed in to allow the spirits to be seen easier on screen, as the images are so fleeting. You can hear when Roger selects a word, as the Ovilus talks in its weird old-fashioned computer voice. I relay the words he says, to acknowledge each new word he chooses. I am just about to give up looking for Poppy's spirit, when Roger says, *dog*, on the Ovilus. This makes me pick up the camera again and resume the search. Just after Roger says *shoot*, a stick figure very briefly appears, apparently moving, in front of the curtain by the front door – exactly where Peggy is looking! I am sure this is Poppy's spirit, which Peggy can see, and Roger made me keep filming in order to see it – he knew she was there, and he encouraged me to keep looking. Well done, Roger, you continue to amaze me.

I didn't realise just how good this video is until I re-examined it whilst writing this chapter, seven months after I filmed it. Roger has spoiled us with everything he has shown us on camera, as he is still continuing to do as I write this.

I hope when you watch this video you can share in the utter amazement that I feel, with exactly what it is we are seeing. Who would have thought that a green stick figure could be so utterly incredible? What that incredible stick figure is making visible to us is an invisible spirit, or soul, of our loved ones. This isn't some zany ghost hunt, briefly showing a spirit (or glitch?) by an incredibly sophisticated bit of physical technology and software (the SLS camera), but a real vision into the afterlife, showing my discarnate father-in-law, Roger, and now my discarnate beloved spaniel, Poppy. Seeing their actual souls through the electronic eyes of a piece of kit which was designed to allow computer gamers to play their games, is an incredible unintended ability that those very clever Microsoft engineers created over a decade ago. Thanks, Microsoft, your obsolete technology has just proved to humankind, on camera, that there is an afterlife. For that, I, and hopefully many other people, will be eternally grateful.

Everything written in the chapter above was what I thought at the time that I wrote it, however, many months later, once we had got Edie and she was still a youngish puppy, something happened which made me have to rethink everything that I had thought up until that point. Caroline was in the kitchen one night with Edie, while it was dark outside. Suddenly, Edie started behaving very, very strangely, barking in a seemingly fearful way, looking quite frightened. Caroline turned on her phone to video Edie and then showed me the video. After studying it, I couldn't believe what I was seeing. Edie was looking out of the door into the garden outside, into the dark; just outside the door she was looking at something on the patio. That something, I am as certain as I can be, is the ghost of Poppy. I have read plenty of books about animal ghosts and they are surprisingly fairly common and well documented. Studying this video really carefully, I can see Poppy's ghost looking at Edie through the glass, and Edie reciprocating the look to the ghost of Poppy. Edie is very confused, scared and submissive in her demeanour. Poppy is definitely giving her the evil eye, telling her that she is still the boss. We always knew that Edie would be *second best*; Poppy would still be *the best*.

This was such an unexpected turn of events for me as I thought I understood everything to date, but clearly, I didn't. The facts had changed, or more accurately, new facts had come to light, and I struggled for some time to work out all the implications and exactly where things stood in the light of these new facts. I knew that Edie's character was different to Poppy's, so I was already slightly struggling to fully believe that Poppy had reincarnated into Edie. Rereading my books had reminded me that a reincarnated animal won't have the same character as the deceased animal, but rather a blend of the deceased animal's soul and the new animal's soul. The excellent medium Ali Mather had told us that Poppy was still earthbound, meaning she was still around us. This apparition of Poppy does tend to prove that she really is very literally still around us, and presumably that does mean that she didn't reincarnate into Edie as I had first thought.

One big question for me in the light of this was whether or not the stick figure spirit in our living room, who I regularly see, was Poppy. Was it Poppy or not? Well, it's quite possible that it was Poppy, and Roger did seem to confirm that with the Ovilus, with the words that he used: *poppa, dog,* etc. I do, however, think now that this second spirit who I see regularly in the living room could be Joan. It could be that this spirit is sometimes Joan, and sometimes was Poppy. I know this sounds confusing, and it really is. A lot of the experts in the books I read do say spirits can be in more than one place at once, and I know that spirits can go inside of a person (as Roger did when Ali Mather the medium was doing a reading – she explained to us that this is how mediums sometimes get the best messages from the spirit, as it blends with the medium), so there is definitely some sort of overlap. Possibly there could be a blend of spirits; possibly Joan and Poppy both hang out in the same place in the living room, next to where Caroline normally sits. Poppy was devoted to Caroline, especially in her later years, and Joan was such a loving mother to Caroline, maybe the two spirits are jostling to have the prime location in the living room next to Caroline's place.

So, what should we make of this very confusing situation? Well, there are several things that we do know for certain: One is that Roger did try and comfort Caroline and me as soon as Poppy died; we could see him right above Poppy on the settee. He did acknowledge Poppy on the Ovilus by using some keywords. We also know that a spirit does quite often reside in front of the standard lamp next to where Caroline normally sits. The bizarre twist of actually seeing the ghost of Poppy on camera, which is corroborated by Edie's very strange behaviour, does confirm what Ali Mather told us, that Poppy is still earthbound. The only area of doubt is who this spirit is in front of the standard lamp. Although I had been getting the feeling that it was Poppy, I do think now it was Joan, or maybe they do alternate. Whichever it is, it doesn't really matter. Unfortunately, Roger hasn't managed to confirm one way or the other.

For any readers who are wanting to track down their deceased loved one, as I've said before, just go with your instincts. When something new and unexpected crops up, as with us with Poppy's ghost suddenly appearing, then hard as it might be at the time, embrace it and try and work out what the new information is adding to your existing knowledge so far.

This is possibly one of the biggest lessons of trying to track down Roger's spirit; even when you think you understand the situation, suddenly something you haven't foreseen occurs, and you have to reassess where you are. Later chapters in the book describe some more very unexpected turns of events, when everything I believed at the time was turned on its head, and I had to work out what it meant, and how I would deal with it. Everything described in this book is how it really transpired, so I hope you, the reader, appreciate what an amazing rollercoaster of revelations we have been on, courtesy of Joan and Roger, and Poppy.

We all know that life has its twists and turns and things don't happen how we expect or plan them to occur. It has become obvious that these same twists and turns occur as the afterlife is revealed to us. This does make the whole story even more incredible, and I have metaphorically been sat on the edge of my seat throughout this whole fantastic story that we have been witness to. I never cease to be amazed at everything that we have been shown. Seeing is definitely believing in my case, and definitely, I'm sure, in most people's cases. I do believe everything I've seen, once I have comprehended just what it is I am looking at. I believe that trusting my instincts in my nascent psychic abilities has paid dividends, and I am 100% certain that Roger the teacher has been on a mission to give me a lesson on what he now knows about the afterlife so far. He has taken hold of the baton from Joan and run with it. Poppy too has given us a priceless lesson, alongside Roger's lessons. I'm just so grateful to them all for taking the trouble to show us these incredible, mystical things.

I really hope that you, the reader, do appreciate the dedication shown by Roger, started by Joan, aided by Poppy, that has brought this story to us, and now via this book, to you. I am so keen to share this story with you and for you to understand that it is real. If this story was fictional, it would be thought too far-fetched and unbelievable. But this story is real, and although it might seem unbelievable, Roger is doing everything he can to help us to believe it.

Isn't it just pretty mind-bending to think that Roger, the avowed nonbeliever, is showing us that there really is an afterlife, which turns out to confirm that all conventional religions are actually based on truth? I, for one, stopped believing in my Catholic faith when I was a teenager, simply because it seemed ridiculously far-fetched, but now I'm being shown that this far-fetched religion was based on reality, and I was wrong.

Even though Roger has communicated with us using the Ovilus talking dictionary, he can only say the occasional word that is definitely correct, but sometimes he comes out with words that don't seem to make sense. For this reason, very soon after Roger started showing on the SLS camera, I realised that I would be keen to get a medium to communicate with Roger, while we had him showing on camera. Initially, I had great trouble getting any medium interested in trying this out for us.

One medium was positively furious that I was even trying to do this, she said I might trap Roger here on Earth, and it was totally unfair of me to even attempt this.

The very first medium who agreed, and who was actually keen on trying what I was asking, was Ali Mather. In the next chapter you can read all about Ali Mather and what she did for us, and how superb she was.

Later chapters describe other mediums who we got to try and help us communicate with Roger. I have read several times that the more you communicate with the spirit, the more you want: it's never enough. This really does seem to be true. In reading the later chapters on mediums, you will be interested to know that some have been fantastic, whereas one very famous medium was definitely not fantastic. As always, it's been a very hard but important lesson, we need to trust our own instincts. Whatever new facts come to light, we need to deal with them. Joan and Roger's story has been utterly spellbinding, not knowing where the next step might lead us.

Stop Press!

Since writing this book, after Jo had edited it and I was about to send the manuscript to the publishers, a very sad thing happened to Edie's best friend, Rex. Although tragic, it is remarkably illuminating from an evidential viewpoint.

Rex was a cocker spaniel, just a few months older than Edie. Right from the start, when they first met, they loved playing together. They were fairly evenly matched, although Rex was a little quicker. Unfortunately, Rex was a very difficult dog to control, so his owner, Mike, used to keep him on a very long trainer lead all the time, as otherwise he would suddenly run off into the distance and be gone for ages, until Mike finally managed to find him. He would run out of sight, into fields adjacent to our local park and beyond. Several times we helped Mike find Rex, as we traipsed through the ploughed farmers' fields that Rex would endlessly traverse in massive, non-stop circuits.

Gradually Mike became more confident and began to release Rex from his lead, in the hope that he would run with Edie and that he wouldn't go off by himself into the distance, but this policy wasn't always successful.

The last few months Rex seemed to be calming down and getting better at recall, Mike always having a ready supply of Rex's favourite treats to tempt him back. Even so, he would still suddenly run off and chase a pigeon, and sometimes catch it, at which point he would not let go of it no matter what Mike tried in order to loosen his jaws' iron grip on the dead bird. I couldn't believe just how strong Rex's bite and his will were.

Recently Rex had taken to chasing the local deer who lived near the park.

The last time we saw Rex was on a Friday when Edie and Rex had a lovely run together in the park. All seemed well as we left for home, while Mike, ever dedicated to Rex, stayed on to give him an extra-long run.

The next time we came to the park was on the Sunday. As soon as we let Edie off the lead, she behaved differently to her normal self. She just ran and ran around the park, in very large sweeping circuits, running off into the distance, but thankfully coming back, just visible to us at all times. Edie never behaved like this normally. She would usually stay close to us, only running in short spurts, especially when we threw the ball for her. Today was totally different. Caroline and I both agreed that she suddenly had Rex's character in her today. She never stopped running until we left the park for home.

Later that day, Mike sent Caroline a message: Rex had died on the Friday, just after we had seen them in the park. He had seen a deer and chased it as per usual. Tragically, the deer ran onto the nearby motorway, with Rex in pursuit.

Poor Rex. Poor Mike. Mike was devoted to Rex, a fantastic spaniel-dad.

Poor Edie – she's lost her best friend.

The big question we're unable to answer for certain is whether or not Edie was running around the park on the Sunday with Rex's spirit.

Did she see his spirit, and they both ran around together, as Rex always did? If so, did Rex know he was no longer a physical dog? After a sudden death, spirits don't always realise they've died – is this how Rex is now?

Perhaps Rex is earthbound to be with Mike. Maybe he saw Edie in the park, and decided he wanted to play with her, as usual. We know Poppy is earthbound, staying around us – we've seen her on video, when we know that Edie saw her.

Whatever the explanation, this is both tragic and fascinating in equal measure.

Whichever way you look at it, this is one more bit of concrete proof of life after death. What amazing things our beloved dogs are able to prove to us!

Chapter 6

Ali Mather, Top UK Medium

As soon as I got the electronic ghost hunting equipment and I saw Roger on the SLS camera, I realised that his communication through the Ovilus, although at times very impressive, had room for improvement. It's very true that the more you get, the more you want, it's never enough, and although the visual side on camera was pretty much as good as I could ever want, I did realise that I wanted a proper conversation with Roger. I knew this wasn't possible, but I realised at this point that maybe a medium could speak for Roger in response to any questions that we might have for him. I was desperate just to chat with him and hear what he had to say.

I searched for local mediums on Google and there were a few, although not that many, and I contacted all of the ones who weren't too far away to tell them what we had found on camera, and to ask if they would help us in our quest to speak to Roger's spirit while we filmed him on camera. Most mediums didn't respond at all, no doubt thinking I was a complete nutcase. One medium responded in a really irate manner, saying I was being totally unreasonable and reckless, risking Roger's spiritual health. She said I was going to trap him here on Earth, when he could otherwise move on to his rightful place in the spiritual world – wherever that was. She was vehement in her criticism of what I was doing. I was utterly shocked and taken aback – I really hadn't thought I was being so potentially reckless with Roger's very existence in Heaven. It made me question myself – was I misguided, and was I actually a complete nutcase?

I was beginning to really doubt what I was trying to do. Thank goodness, just in time to restore my faith in human nature, one medium did respond positively: Ali Mather. She was totally sympathetic to what we were trying to do, and she was totally familiar with all the equipment that I was using. I booked a session with her at her house, but it was many weeks away, so I had an anxious wait as I eagerly anticipated just what Ali might be able to achieve.

In the subsequent week or two from speaking to Ali, I had a couple of other mediums agree to try communicating with Roger. These two both came to our house before Ali Mather's appointment took place. Both these mediums were lovely people, but unfortunately, even though Roger was there on camera trying his best, they were unable to communicate with him. We just knew their answers were not Roger communicating with us. I was now a lot less hopeful that Ali Mather would be able to achieve anything positive at all – maybe I was aiming for the impossible, as I so often do.

When the day finally came to see Ali Mather, we got to her house and she showed us to the room where she does her readings. We sat down at a small table while Ali made us some coffees. I turned the equipment on straightaway while we waited for the coffee to brew, and lo and behold, Roger was there in the room on camera all the time while we waited with bated breath to see what might occur when the reading got underway. After about 10 minutes, Ali came in with the coffees and as she walked in front of Roger he briefly disappeared, then briefly reappeared in front of her chair. As soon as she sat down, Roger was no longer visible in the room, and he didn't show up on camera again for the whole session.

Although he didn't show, Ali reassured me that Roger's spirit had blended with her own, and she was channelling him, which means that he was within her, which would give her the best possible communication with him.

Her reading lasted for more than one hour, which was a combination of us chatting to confirm certain things, then she would break off for a minute or two to explain a certain point, as this was all new to us. She had strong feelings from several people coming through to her, including two women – one having cancer, who Caroline didn't recognise, and the other having heart problems and a weakness down one side, which could have been caused by a stroke. Caroline initially thought she didn't recognise this person, but I told Ali that Caroline's mum had had a stroke some years prior to her death, but she had recovered completely from it – Ali confirmed this probably was her. She described this woman's death as being sudden, without warning, and connected to her heart problem – this is exactly how Joan died.

Ali also had a couple of men come through. One of them had a sore back and a painful leg, which Caroline didn't think could be her dad, but in his last year or two, he did have very swollen legs relating to his heart problem, and he did have a very sore behind. Although this seemed slightly amusing, it really was quite a serious thing, and Roger did flash the K2 meter to acknowledge that this was true.

Ali also said this person seemed to have a very dry mouth, possibly linked to diabetes, which confirmed it was Roger – he had had diabetes for years, but also he didn't drink enough liquid and it was a constant battle in his last year, trying to get him to drink enough. Ali felt this person had various stomach problems; this was very true of Roger. He did have major stomach-related problems which became very complicated, and did eventually contribute to his physical downfall. Initially it seemed to start with an abscess on his skin above his navel, and by the time any of us saw it, it was really severe. His local doctor completely failed to appreciate the severity of it, so by the time we saw it, I instantly knew it was necessary for Roger to go to hospital.

He ended up after a number of operations with a colostomy, because the bowel was too badly damaged to be mended. The colostomy was just too difficult for Roger to cope with – he couldn't eat properly due to the high position of the colostomy within the bowel, and when he was home it was an impossible situation for him. Some months later he had the colostomy reversed successfully by the same amazing surgeon.

As the reading with Ali Mather progressed, when I explained to her about the colostomy as she was feeling major stomach problems, Roger flashed the K2 meter lights really strongly to acknowledge that this was one of the major medical issues he had.

Ali Mather's reading was so accurate in so many ways, but we did help guide her messages and feelings she was getting from Roger, as she could not quite understand one or two things he was telling her. It was a very complicated medical situation. Once explained she could then move on, and Roger could give her the next part of his intricate story.

One of the biggest questions I had for Roger was whether he did believe in an afterlife or not, prior to finding himself in the afterlife. He told Ali that he really couldn't get his head around it – he really hadn't been able to imagine that it could possibly be real, so he didn't believe in it. It was such an amazing surprise for him when he found there was an afterlife, and she said, "He was like someone who had just discovered religion." This is exactly the feeling I get from Roger. He definitely is trying to tell us all his story, because he finds what he has recently discovered so incredible.

He also told Ali that he was very grateful for all the help the family had given him, and he knows that he didn't thank them enough when he was here. Maybe he took it for granted too much, but now he is in the afterlife it is easier for him to thank everyone for doing what they did.

During the reading Ali mentioned a dog, and she didn't quite know what the situation was. We told her that Poppy our beloved spaniel had died just two weeks ago, and then she was able to understand what Roger was telling her: that the dog was stubborn and Roger couldn't get her spirit to go with him to the afterlife. Ali said the dog wanted to stay with us, and so she is earthbound, still around us at home. Caroline knew this would be the case, as Poppy was so loyal to us and wouldn't leave us. We told Ali that on the day she died on the settee, Roger's spirit was visible on the SLS camera above Poppy, while he comforted both us and Poppy. Caroline and I were totally distraught, finding her death possibly harder to deal with than a human death, which seems rather bizarre, but is totally true. Ali fully understands this, as she is such a dog person herself, with several rehomed and foster dogs of her own. She is totally dedicated to her dogs.

The video for this chapter is an edited version of the very long video we took at Ali's house nearly 18 months ago. The first few minutes show Roger's spirit in the room while we waited for Ali to make our coffees. The next part shows various sections of the reading, and especially shows the occasions when Roger flashes the K2 meter to underline things that are being said that he strongly agrees with.

So, this reading with Ali Mather, once I had fully digested it, proved to me that a good medium could communicate with Roger, and give us some detailed answers which the Ovilus would never be able to do.

Over subsequent weeks, I communicated with Ali via email and told her that I was writing a book about Roger and Joan and everything they were doing in the afterlife, especially having got our attention with their amazing signs, which Joan initiated, and Roger continued. Having got the electronic equipment and then been able to see Joan's and Roger's spirits on camera, I had the very strong feeling that their story had to be told in a book, which I felt Roger was organising. Roger's whole life was to do with books – they were his main passion, and he had written some non-fiction books himself. I knew it was going to be a lot of work, but Ali Mather was so positive and supportive of what I was attempting. She really gave me some good advice to help me to achieve success in this very difficult pursuit. She was in total agreement that Roger was initiating this whole project, I just had to stay positive and focused and it would be successful in the end. She sent me a very inspirational video to watch called *The Secret*, which is almost like an over-the-top instructional sales video; it tells you to visualise what your goal is, and the more you visualise it and visualise yourself achieving your goal, the more likely you are to achieve it. Whatever you set your mind to, if you stay positive, you will achieve it. I keep this advice at the forefront of my mind, and every time I've been tempted to give up because it seems such a daunting task, I just remember that I have committed to Roger to see it through, to get his book published and to allow as many people as possible to read his and Joan's amazing, almost unbelievable, story.

Since meeting Ali Mather initially, she has become a very good friend, especially to Caroline. Unbeknown to me, Caroline had contacted Ali some months ago when we were having a particularly hard time with one of our sons. Ali was able to help Caroline enormously, and to send some spiritual healing to him, which definitely seemed to help the situation. Many months on, this awkward situation does seem to be well under control. We really are grateful to Ali for everything she has done and continues to do for us.

Some weeks ago, one of our other sons was suddenly in a very difficult situation. One of his good friends who was terminally ill with cancer, died. Tracy was an older lady, almost our age. In fact, she had been Caroline's friend initially, then Patrick had become very friendly with her for many years. Towards the end, she asked him to take charge of all her earthly affairs, which he promised he would. Patrick is a very good soul, and he committed to supporting Tracy in every way he could. He was with her in the hospital at the end, but she died just as he had left for the day, so instantly he returned to be with her. It will have been a massive shock for him, as this was his first encounter with death face to face.

Just a few weeks later Patrick had a second encounter with death, when his fiancée's father died at home and he was the one to discover it. Bob also had terminal cancer, and Patrick just happened to be the one checking up on him. When he walked into the house, into the living room, he found Bob dead.

Encountering death for the first time is always a big shock for anyone, but to do it twice in just a few weeks must be doubly hard. I wasn't even sure if Patrick believed in life after death. I suspected he didn't. When we had first discovered Roger's spirit on camera, I had told all the children about what we had found, and that Christmas when we first got the equipment when some of the children and grandchildren were round at our house, I got the equipment out, having already shown them the videos we had taken of their granny and grandad at the cemetery. Roger did show on camera with them, but it was difficult initially to be sure, because with so many living people in shot, it was hard to discern if Roger was there or not. I'm not sure if the children believed what we were telling them – I think they thought we had taken leave of our senses. (As so many people did, and some still do. I must admit, on the face of it, it really does sound totally bizarre and impossible, but as I have to keep reminding myself, *it really is true*!)

With Patrick coming face to face with death for the first time, I realised I should try and help him to come to terms with what he was discovering life is all about. This all happened just within the last couple of months, so I suggested he might find it helpful to meet Ali Mather and have a reading with her, to see if Tracy and Bob might come through with messages. If this were to happen, then it might be comforting for Patrick to know that there is life after death. Another thing I was keen to try, and to answer my own queries, was for Ali Mather to do some *Past Life Regression*, to see if Patrick had lived before in a previous life. I was really intrigued, because when Patrick was a child, he used to talk about his previous life as a man on a sailing ship. When speaking to him in recent years he couldn't remember this, so he said that if Past Life Regression could work for Patrick, then I was fascinated to find out whether he would find one of his past lives was as a sailor.

I arranged for Patrick and me to go and see Ali Mather. The plan was that I would try Past Life Regression for myself, with Patrick, as it's as easy for two people to do it at the same time as it is for one, according to Ali. After this session, Patrick alone would have a reading with Ali to see who, if anyone, she might get messages from.

We started the Past Life Regression process while Ali told us what to do in order to get us into a suitably meditative state of mind. She told us to visualise a whole series of scenes in our mind's eye, which culminated in us ending up in a beautiful place by a big tree in the centre of the Earth. At this point we were directed to go through a door in a round building, down a spiral ramp, through another door into a hotel corridor, and then into three hotel rooms off this corridor, one at a time. There is a lot more detail to this of course, but these are the salient points that I can remember.

I managed to visualise, following all of the instructions until I entered the first hotel room. At that point I could not visualise anything else. We were supposed to see a mirror in the room, and in that mirror, we would see the person who we had been in a previous life and we would have been able to talk to them, to find out about that life.

After leaving Ali's house after several hours, Patrick and I each made our own way home. I spoke to him a few days later to find out what had happened in his sessions. He had managed to get the Past Life Regression to work very well. The first past life he had lived was as a man with a weathered face, wearing a suit, and there were ropes, and it was stormy. When I asked

Patrick where the ropes were, he said the man was holding a coil of very thick rope. I asked him what sort of era this would have been, and he said probably 100 to 150 years ago. I asked him if he thought the man could be a sailor, and he agreed – he had wondered that himself. This all makes sense to me as he mentioned *stormy*, which obviously the weather could be while on a sailing ship, or at least when by the sea. The rope could well have been a rope from a sailing ship. In this era, working men often did wear suits, as in those days they didn't have the sort of protective clothing that we have got used to in recent times. Patrick did agree that this probably was a sailor, and this did seem to confirm that what Patrick used to say as a child was true, that he had lived before in a previous life as a sailor, or at least, on board a sailing ship.

The other two past lives Patrick wasn't sure about, and he didn't feel comfortable exploring those in any detail.

The reading he had later with Ali was very revealing. Tracy did come through to him. He could tell it was Tracy from Ali's description of her character, being very, very stubborn, of being frightened of dying with her illness, and not trusting what the doctors were telling her. She was also very grateful to Patrick for looking after her and taking care of everything once she had died. All this apparently is exactly what Tracy was like. A big surprise was that Tracy had a big dog with her. In life she didn't have her own dog, but Patrick recognised that this was his dog, Bella, who had died in the last year or two, and she apologised to Patrick for weeing everywhere, which she did in her last few months.

Another person who made contact through Ali was Bob who said a few things that indicated it could only have been Bob.

Patrick was 100% certain that everything that happened at Ali Mather's proved beyond doubt life after death. Although he said that he had already believed in some sort of afterlife, he found the day with Ali really comforting and helpful. Patrick's fiancée is very keen to have her own reading with Ali in the next few weeks, once her dad's funeral is out of the way. She believes in all of this medium business anyway and knows she will benefit when she feels up to it, hopefully very soon.

The editor of this book, Jo, who lives in Australia, has also had a couple of readings from Ali Mather. The first one was last year on FaceTime – Jo in Australia, Ali in the UK. Jo says that was amazingly, surprisingly accurate. She found it quite hard, as it brought up some uncomfortable old memories.

The second reading was just a couple of months ago, when Jo came over to the UK without her husband who had come with her previously, to see Caroline. Caroline organised for a reading at Ali's house. This reading was also spot on, and Jo found it incredibly useful at helping her to sort out some awkward things in her life. The details are as follows:

> My first reading with Ali was beautiful yet emotionally challenging. Although I didn't feel Ali had captured the essence of my beloved grandmother, when she brought my father through it was an entirely different story! I almost felt like it was him I was talking to, not a woman in the UK, 10,000 miles away. Ali spoke of some very simple yet meaningful things – the birds I see, the cigarette smoke I smell and the like. Of course, these things are generic in nature and could be easily attributed to many people. Right? Things then took a serious and much more specific turn. Ali told me he is sorry and he understands now. To my surprise she mentioned, in the exact words, a nasty fight that had occurred many years ago between my father and me. She urged me not to feel guilty about it. How could she possibly have known about this? I was too ashamed of my role in this argument my whole life to mention this disagreement to ANYONE! Ali also said he was sorry for his part in a separate series of events

which caused me lifelong trauma. The details she relayed were too specific to be "guesses". Sadly, the conversation dredged up old feelings and memories that I wasn't prepared to deal with. That would come later.

My second reading with Ali took place in England. My grandmother had always said we have guardian angels looking over us, helping, guiding and protecting us. I was very interested in Spirit Guides and wondered who might be looking out for me. It was no surprise that Granny and Dad came through immediately and strongly. Granny seemed more like herself this time and Dad was still Dad – his dominant personality has certainly stayed with him into the afterlife. I was so pleased when another cherished family member came through. My message to him was, "I'm sorry. Tell him I'm sorry." His message for me was, "The guilt you feel is not yours to bear." As the reading went on Ali became more and more clear with regard to the situation my father was sorry about in the first reading. As Ali introduced me to my non-familial spirit guides, it was like she kept being drawn back to my father and the incredulousness of that situation pestered her and niggled at her. She could now see why the first reading had jangled my nerves and for me, this was validating and comforting. The time in between readings meant I had time and space to reflect and sort through my thoughts and feelings. With a new sense of clarity, I could finally let go of the past and move forward. Thank you, Ali.

The non-familial Spirit Guide section of the reading was remarkably on point. To say I was amazed is an understatement. The discussion and information Ali provided was much more detailed than I am presenting here but this brief outline gives you the gist. In addition to my family who watch over me I have 4 Spirit Guides who direct, assist and comfort me.

The Healing Guide. I'm a fit and healthy person with a couple of very specific issues. Ali was on point each time.

The Career Guide – perfect explanation of my "cushy job". Ali made many salient points and I could relate to each one. She said a change would be coming next year – at the time of the reading no change was on the horizon.

The Learning Guide – coming to stir up the learning. Very interesting as I am a lifelong learner, always looking for the next thing. On point.

The Music Man – A highly specific guide sent for a range of purposes. Several points made. All of them extremely relatable.

The tarot cards – a major change in home and job. "Downsizing to be more financially comfortable." This is very interesting. At the time of this reading, I had no interest or desire to move house. However, 3 months after this reading my husband approached me with the idea to sell up and downsize so we would be mortgage free. Our home is currently on the market and we are looking to relocate to a beautiful seaside area 250 miles north. I guess I'll be looking for that new job after all.

Ali had told me when I first spoke to her, that she had had her own personal afterlife experience – when she had died, in hospital, and then been resuscitated. I spoke to her recently to find out more details and asked her how her spiritual powers became apparent.

As a small child, Ali had always had an imaginary friend, which is very common with children. She says that in the dark she could always see people-shaped things in the room. Every year she used to have a dream in which her aunt was coming to her in the dream and talking to her, but around the age of 12 she said she was going to have to stop coming, because she wasn't allowed to come any more. In her late teens, Ali could see various relatives, but she found it more of a nuisance than anything. She started doing Tarot readings and found they were accurate. She always used to see things out of the corner of her eye, which she says is because you're not seeing it with your physical eye, but with your Third Eye, which is a Chakra in the middle of your forehead, and it is this which allows you spiritually to see all around you.

Ali's elder sister has spiritual abilities too, but her middle sister doesn't. Her dad used to have strange dreams, so he might have been spiritual, but her mum didn't have any spiritual abilities, so possibly Ali's abilities came from her father's side of the family.

Ali's amazing experience of dying was nine years ago at the Alexander Football Ground in Crewe, at a Mind, Body and Spirit event. She was away for the weekend, and on the Saturday night when she got back to the hotel, she was feeling under the weather. She had a slight sore throat, couldn't get warm, and on the Sunday morning she couldn't get out of bed. The hotel called an ambulance, and she was taken to the local hospital in Crewe. She was in her bed in the hospital, and couldn't get the nurses' attention, so she got out of bed to try and find a nurse. She then collapsed in the corridor. At this point everything went black, but Ali could hear a distant voice of someone asking for help, and she was starting to get annoyed with whoever it was calling out. Eventually she realised it was Ali herself, asking for help, but her conscious mind was elsewhere, floating in total blackness, totally separate from her own physical body. This all seemed like it was only 30 seconds from start to finish, but Ali knows that it was quite a few minutes, as when she did eventually come round in her physical body again she was back in her bed with a lot of nurses and doctors around her, and all sorts of equipment that they had used to resuscitate her. A brain scan and lumbar punctures confirmed that she had bleeding on the brain, but a more detailed scan two or three days later revealed there was no longer any bleeding on the brain at all. The doctors couldn't understand this, but Ali puts it down to a thousand people who were giving her distance healing or praying for her. The doctors were sceptical, but Ali thinks this whole episode was a lesson for her from the Universe, to allow her to experience death for herself, so that when she gives terminally ill people a reading, she fully understands what they are due to experience. Her own mother was to die just a few months after this incident, so she is sure that her own brief death experience was arranged as an important life lesson for her.

Ali found the experience so incredible, peaceful and pleasant that next time she will be very happy to pass over to the afterlife without any worries or hesitation. She won't be frightened but will be keen to go.

To see Ali's extensive range of services, view her website: www.alimather.co.uk

Chapter 7

Stephen Holbrook, UK's Premier Psychic Medium

After Roger died in April 2022, he came through at a Stephen Holbrook evening at Drax Social Club with a 100% accurate message. Unfortunately, we never thought to record the message. Since that time, when we go and see Stephen Holbrook, we do record the evening so that if anything amazing happens, we've got it to listen to and refer back to.

Three weeks after Roger's death, Caroline, together with Alison her sister and her husband, Colin, and myself, went to see Stephen Holbrook. We had been planning to go and see him anyway, but with Roger having died so recently, we decided there was a good chance he might come through with a message. Several years previously when Colin's dad had died, Colin had felt compelled for some reason to see Stephen Holbrook when he saw an advert in the local paper for one of his shows. He'd never seen him before, but Colin's dad came through with a totally accurate message which amazed Colin.

So, it was Colin who introduced us to Stephen Holbrook, and we had seen him a few times before Roger died. Caroline and I had never had anyone personal to us come through at one of these events. Even though we would have loved to have Joan come through, she never had.

Joan had given us loads of signs after she died, like the TVs turning on, lights turning on, and a very strange incident with a bird of prey; a kestrel flew around us twice, at low level, while we walked at Sandal Castle a couple of days after she had died. So, we half expected her to try and talk to us through Stephen Holbrook, but for whatever reason, she never did.

When Roger came through soon after he had died, it was slightly surprising, but we were so grateful that he did. As Roger had been so adamant that he didn't believe in an afterlife – not just that he didn't believe in it, but that there definitely wasn't one – it was more than a little strange that he came through with his amazing message. Maybe he felt guilty for having told everyone there was no afterlife, and then after his death, when he finds that there is, he probably felt compelled to set the record straight, and let us know that there was an afterlife after all, and that he was happy there.

Seven months after Roger died, once we started using the electronic equipment to track his spirit down, which turned out to be so incredibly productive and revealing, I straightaway sent Stephen Holbrook links to Roger's videos of his appearances with the SLS camera. Stephen was very complimentary with how incredible these videos were, and how amazing Roger was. When I realised that Roger was speaking through the Ovilus device, and coming out with some very relevant words, although not every word was relevant, I asked Stephen if he would do an experiment with us whereby we could film Roger on the SLS camera, with Stephen present, and we could ask Roger questions which Roger might answer through Stephen. I thought this would be groundbreaking, and if it worked it would make Roger's appearances on camera even more incredible.

Unfortunately for us, Stephen said that he doesn't do personal appearances. He doesn't feel comfortable doing one-to-one sessions, so he would not try this experiment with us.

I was very disappointed, because I thought he would be keen to push the boundaries between mediumship and technology, revealing the spirit. Caroline had warned me that he might well not want to try this experiment with us, so although not totally surprising, I couldn't help but be slightly miffed.

Over the next few months I messaged Stephen a few times, trying new angles to try to persuade him to agree to this experiment. Knowing how keen Stephen is on his various charity fundraising missions, I offered him a very large donation to one of his charities, in the hope that this would sway him to say yes. He still said no.

Convinced that getting a good medium involved would be key to getting some very accurate answers from Roger, I contacted other mediums to try this experiment. Initially, I was getting nowhere: Several mediums wouldn't do it; several mediums didn't even bother to reply. One medium who we saw at the local Spiritualist Church was excellent and came through with a message from Roger at the church. Even she wouldn't try our one-to-one experiment on camera. I did message her more than once, to try to persuade her, but again she would not be persuaded.

One medium who did eventually accept the challenge, and turned out to be fantastic, was Ali Mather. When she agreed to see Roger, her diary was so full that the appointment didn't happen for another couple of months. After she said yes, two other mediums also agreed to try the experiment. When the time came, we ended up seeing three mediums over two consecutive days. Just like the joke about buses, you wait for ages, and then three turn up at once!

Other chapters in this book describe what happened with the various mediums. As already described earlier, Ali Mather, reassuringly, turned out to be excellent.

About six months after Roger died, we went back to Drax Social Club to see if he would come through again with a message for us, like he did three weeks after he died. Each time we see Stephen Holbrook, we never know what to expect – who might come through and who might not. This time, November 2022, I decided to take various items of my parents' along, to see if these trigger objects might persuade them to come through. I suppose it was mainly my dad who I thought might come through. I was wearing his jacket, but I had some of my mum's items on me, such as her athletics medal from when she was at school, her fountain pen, and I had her Funeral Order of Service in my pocket.

When Roger had come through with a superb message six months previously, we hadn't recorded it, so we had to piece together between the four of us after the event exactly what Roger had said to us. We believe that between us we got everything that he said lodged in our memories.

For anyone who hasn't experienced Stephen Holbrook and the incredible messages that come through for friends and relatives, the following is a transcript of the message that came through from my mother.

Stephen: Has somebody just brought the Order of Service card with them for their mum? Is it your mum's Order of Service? Have you got it with you?

Jeremy: Yes.

Stephen: Did you bring it, thinking, "If I take this she might come through?"

Jeremy: Yes.

Stephen: It didn't help! (laughter from the audience)

Stephen: Your mum believed in something after death.

Jeremy: She did, yes.

Stephen: She knew. She used to tell you; she wasn't scared.

Jeremy: Yes.

Stephen: But she wasn't scared because she knew there was something else. But she wants to tell you that you weren't going to bring it at first.

Jeremy: That's right.

Stephen: I know, and do you know what? She's smiling and she's just said, "I'm well again." But I'm going to tell you something; she was very poorly.

Jeremy: Yes, she had dementia.

Stephen: And do you know what? She's just said, "Tell my son it was beautiful how he looked after me." Do you understand?

Jeremy: Yes.

Stephen: And I know you're sad, so I'm just trying, if you can let me hear your voice. She's just said, "You went above and beyond what was expected of you." Who are you?

Caroline: Daughter-in-law.

Stephen: Daughter-in-law? So, you are married to this gentleman? So, he did more than any man would normally do?

Caroline: He did.

Stephen: And you know what? He did things that you thought he wasn't capable of.

Caroline: He didn't want to do them, but he had to.

Stephen: He didn't want to do them, but he did them. And, she's smiling and she's just said, "I want you both to know it was like I've been let out of prison, for me going over here. I'd had enough. Why do I lie there, day in, day out, not knowing where you are?" Do you understand?

Caroline: Yes.

Stephen: She knows exactly where she is, and she's just said, "You haven't grieved yet." Do you understand? You're too sad, I know, but you speak for him, because do you know what, sweetheart? You came here tonight, and you thought: this isn't about me, this is about him. I know you wanted him to have a message. Do you understand?

Caroline: Yes.

Stephen: But I'm going to tell you something; she wanted you to have her ring. I bet you haven't got it, have you?

Caroline: It's at home.

Stephen: It's at home. So, are you having it?

Caroline: Yes.

Stephen: Good. Well, that's alright, that's what she wants. Don't worry, she won't haunt you! (laughter from the audience). And, do you know what? She's smiling and she's just said, "I know how you look after him."

Caroline: Yes, well, he's very lucky (laughter from the audience).

Stephen: And you're a big head (laughter from the audience). You look after him, but do you know what? How long's your dad been gone?

Jeremy: 28 years.

Stephen: I was going to say, he looks younger than your mother (laughter). Okay, how old was he when he died then? – 60s? Late 60s?

Jeremy: 78 (with Caroline's help).

Stephen: Well, I'll tell you, now, you look at your dad, and at 78, you look at your dad and there's no way you'd believe he was 78.

Caroline & Jeremy: No.

Stephen: Would you?

Caroline & Jeremy: No.

Stephen: Because he looks good. And do you know what? Your dad's just said, "I knew she was coming, she was overdue." (laughter) Okay? And do you know something? You came here tonight and you've thought, I won't get a message, there's too many people. Why would I get a message?

Jeremy: That's right.

Stephen: I know it is.

Jeremy: This is his jacket.

Stephen: And that's your dad's jacket. God, you've done everything possible to try and bring him through! Bless you. Well anyway, your dad's jacket, and he's been gone how long?

Jeremy: 28 years.

Stephen: 28 years?

Caroline: Been in the cupboard 28 years.

Stephen: I was going to say; it's going to look trendy soon. And you've got your mum, and you've got the Order of Service, and they're together.

Jeremy: Yes.

Stephen: And that's what you wanted to know. September. Whose anniversary is September?

Jeremy: It could have been their wedding anniversary.

Stephen: I think it's the fifteenth or sixteenth. Does that mean something to you?

Jeremy: It could be, but I'm not sure.

Stephen: How long's your mum been gone?

Jeremy: Err, six years.

Stephen: Six years. I need to leave. Just before I leave you, do you know who Dot or Dorothy is?

Jeremy: No.

Stephen: God bless you. Thank you very much. Goodnight. With your lovely mum, your dad and your jacket and your Order of Service card. Goodnight!

If you listen to the above on the video for this chapter, you will hear how I can barely talk, Caroline having to talk for me a lot of the time. It's such an emotional occasion, having your dead relative talking to you via Stephen, particularly when I really wasn't expecting her to come through that evening. What she said to me was virtually 100% accurate. There were a couple of things I wasn't sure about: I didn't really know what Mum's beliefs were. She was Church of England, but Dad was Catholic, so my brothers and I were brought up Catholic. I assume she believed in an afterlife, as that's what C of E believe, but I don't actually remember talking to her about it.

Where she says I hadn't grieved yet, that was so true, and in fact I hadn't even realised that until she said it. When she died, we had so much going on in our lives with our fish and chip shop business – we were in the process of extending the shop, so with Mum dying in the care home where she lived, that was just one extra bit of stress in my life at the time. I felt I was overwhelmed with *stuff*; she was just one more unwelcome thing happening at that time. It's sad to say, but with her terrible dementia, she had almost ceased to be a real human some years before. It almost seemed pointless, her still being trapped in her body with her failing mind.

I can fully understand her when she says she felt she had been let out of prison – her dementia really was her prison. We had been her prison warders while she lived with us for three and a half years, until we finally, reluctantly, had to put her in a local care home for her last year. The plan had always been that she would stay with us until the very end, but, finally, we realised that she would be better off looked after in the care home. I felt so guilty.

Another point I'm not sure about is the date in September. I subsequently checked this date with my brother – it wasn't my parents' wedding anniversary, and we couldn't find what relevance the date was. I do believe it must have meant something, but exactly what, I just don't know.

To get even more insight into how Stephen gets his messages from the spirits, the following is an email Caroline sent to Stephen on my behalf, in order to ask very precisely how these messages occur: (Rob is Steve's manager and partner.)

Morning Rob and Steve,

I hope the south west bit of the tour is going well, you are posting some beautiful photos?

I am emailing on behalf of Jeremy. I hope you have had time to listen to the audio I sent from when Jeremy's mum came through. With your permission he would like to include it in his book and he has a couple of questions about it, if you wouldn't mind answering.

Order of Service, did you see a picture of it in your mind?

The message you relay from spirits – do you actually hear them speak those words in your head?

When you say there is someone standing behind the person with the message (in this case my mother) do

> you actually see a picture in your mind of them standing there?
> When you ask an audience member to speak to hear their voice, how do you use that to understand if the message is for them?
> Best regards
> Caroline

Here is the reply.

> Hi there,
> Right, Steve has had a listen – and his face was a picture! Talk about cringe *lol!*
> Okay, so here we go!
> Order of Service – yes, I could see an image of one, like in a template form, so I knew what it was, but not what was on it.
> I actually hear the voices speaking to me, it is somewhat muffled at times, but the majority is as clear as a bell.
> I see a form which is not exact, but enough for me to distinguish between male and female, and also to a degree, the rough age.
> I need the voice of the audience member so I can connect the vibration between the spirit and the 'real' person. It's like a radio frequency when fine tuning, if it's not quite exact, it's not a match.
> Hope this is what you need!
> We are away from next week for a fortnight on holiday, can't flipping wait!
> See you soon
> Rob x

Stephen has certainly given me a very clear explanation of how the spirit messages occur, in his answers. It really is totally incredible, and to those of us who are not psychic, it just seems so unbelievable – but one way or another, my mother definitely was giving Stephen her message for him to relay to me and a couple of hundred people in the room.

Eventually, while I was getting rather fed up not knowing how to progress matters with Roger on camera, unbeknown to me, Caroline contacted Stephen Holbrook to ask him if he would let us film at his upcoming Drax event in April 2023. Caroline told Stephen that I would be discreet with the SLS camera, sitting in the audience inconspicuously filming the evening.

When the day came, we arrived very early so that we could be first into the event, in order to get the best seats, which we needed if we were to successfully film the evening. From experiments we had done, I knew that we needed to be within 12 feet of Stephen and the stage where he would be performing, if it was to work at all. We sat in our place for about an hour waiting for the start of the show. When Stephen started, he actually positioned himself on the floor in front of the stage, not on the stage itself as he had done previously when we had seen him. This actually meant that we were well within the 12 feet distance to him when he was on our side of the room. As some of you who are familiar with Stephen will know, he walks around a lot when he is talking to the audience, so at times could well have been out of shot of the SLS camera, which could mean that it might not work.

In the event, we did see spirits on camera. In fact, out of the total 90 minutes performance, 13 minutes of footage showed spirits on the SLS. At the end of this chapter is a link to the video of all these spirits on camera. I hope you will all be amazed yet again at what we were able to film.

Although Roger didn't come through with a message at this show, I am certain that he was there on camera, showing up as a stick figure. A couple of days later when I filmed Roger at home, he did confirm by flashing the K2 EMF meter that he was at the show, but he was unable to come through with a message because there were so many other spirits trying to talk through Stephen – he wasn't able to get a word in edgeways. I had warned Roger prior to the event that he would have to be pushy in order to get his message through. But maybe a year after his amazing message through Stephen, just after he had died, he didn't have the same pushiness or urgency to get his message through this time.

So, on camera at Drax, we see a spirit showing up in front of the stage, just a few feet from Stephen. Then again, next to and slightly behind Stephen. Sometimes the spirit is a jumble of lines. Sometimes it appears to be a recognisable human shape. Often, Stephen will have his own stick figure on him, which is exactly what the SLS camera was designed to do. There are times when the spirit appears to migrate into Stephen and other times when spirits seem to come out from Stephen. It is impossible to explain exactly what is going on, but I know that definitely *something* is going on. There definitely are spirits showing on camera. I know these aren't glitches in the way the camera functions, as sceptics on the internet insist is the case.

When Stephen concludes the first half of the show and he talks about his books that are available to purchase, a spirit shows itself in front of the stage at floor level, and then it goes up onto the stage in front of the curtain. Caroline thinks that is her dad, because Roger was so keen on books; he would be bound to be helping Stephen, to point out these books of his. When Stephen comes over to us at this point, we tell him that spirits did show up on camera. Stephen is amazed, and keeps saying, "You're joking!" The K2 meter keeps flashing while we are talking to him, so perhaps that was Roger emphasising that he was around.

In the second half of the show two spirits are showing in front of the stage, and one goes under the stool and stays for four minutes looking at our camera, it seems. The other spirit is next to the stool, appearing rather strange, then it disappears. The one under the stool seems to be waving to us. I think this is Roger, because he is looking at us with the SLS camera, and probably Roger would be the only one in the room who knows what the SLS camera does, and who knows who Caroline and me are.

Stephen could be quite some distance from us, talking to other people in the room, but the spirit of Roger stays under the stool, seemingly waving to Caroline and myself. At one point Stephen walks behind the stool and spirit, and then the spirit seems to attach to Stephen. This spirit of Roger had initially seemed to come from Stephen, and after being on camera for about four minutes, the spirit seems to go back onto Stephen.

It could be that the camera is unable to tell where the spirit is exactly, but it could be the spirit is showing through Stephen. At various times several spirits show up very briefly. After this four-minute period when Stephen moves the stool, the spirit appears to get dragged along with the stool. There's lots of K2 meter flashing while the little spirit is next to Stephen.

When this spirit stops showing, the K2 meter lights still keep flashing, then a spirit appears again on stage behind Stephen, and again, lots of K2 meter flashing which goes on for about 40 seconds. This spirit, I think, could actually be the mother of a lady in the audience Stephen is talking to. The attitude of the spirit, and the angle it appears, suggest to me that the spirit is focusing on Stephen. He says to the lady in the audience that this woman, her mother, tried to come through earlier, but the woman wouldn't put up her hand. Stephen asks if 25 December means anything to this lady, and she says it was her mum's birthday. The message this woman gives to her daughter through Stephen, is, "I'm not going to keep trying, you know. You need to put your hand up." When the spirit disappears, that turns out to be the last spirit appearance on the SLS camera of the evening.

So, who is this man who gives thousands of people a year these ludicrously accurate messages from their loved ones, from beyond the grave?

Stephen was born in Wakefield and grew up in his home village of Walton, just outside the city. He had a very strong link to his grandfather, John, whom he hung out with a lot.

Stephen's dad managed the Wakefield Theatre Club, and often Stephen and his grandad would go to the club the morning after a performance and help tidy up, while his grandad would collect discarded cigarette ends in order to reuse the tobacco for his own roll-ups. His grandad had a dog which Stephen loved. One day Stephen was walking the dog along the pavement on a lead when suddenly the dog pulled out of his hand, ran across the road chasing a cat, and instantly got killed. Stephen was so upset.

One minute the dog was there full of life, the next it was dead, silent and covered in blood. This upset Stephen for a long time; he'd never seen death before.

In the early '70s, Stephen's grandfather became seriously ill. Stephen didn't know the whole story: he just knew that his grandad was very poorly in hospital. At this time, Stephen was in his early teens. One night Stephen awoke in the middle of the night to find his grandfather sitting on the end of his bed. When he asked him what he was doing there, he gave a smile and told him he'd just popped in to say goodbye.

Stephen closed his eyes, and then when he reopened them, his grandad had gone. He was very upset. He looked at the clock to see what time it was – just before four o'clock in the morning. When he got up the next morning for school, his mum realised that something was wrong. He seemed to be tired and fed up. He told her that he'd had a visit from Grandad at four in the morning. She gave him a funny look. He went to school as normal about 8:30. At five to nine, she had a call from the hospital to say that Grandad had died, at 3:55 a.m.

At school, Stephen's schoolwork began to suffer because he couldn't concentrate properly. He found it difficult to hear what the teachers were saying, due to voices in his head.

At the age of 16, Stephen went to see his doctor about these voices. He told Stephen there was nothing he could prescribe, but if he wanted a cure, then Stephen should go to his local Spiritualist Church. He told Stephen not to tell anyone that he had told him to do this.

He became a member of the Church in the mid-80s, where he found that he was a natural clairaudient medium. Stephen learnt how to mute the voices and tune in to what they were saying. Over a couple of years, he made great progress. Around this time, he met his future wife, Caroline. Once married, they went on to have three children. Stephen's reputation grew and he had lots of clients, but he didn't feel happy doing one-to-one readings.

Stephen's sister Joanne had a boyfriend, Paul, who was a DJ at a nightclub in Wakefield. Stephen gave Paul a one-to-one reading. A couple of things Stephen described subsequently turned out to be true; Paul was very impressed. When a visiting medium to the nightclub failed to show up as expected, Paul recommended that Stephen take her place. At 17, Stephen went on the public stage for the first time. He knew most people in the room, but it went well, even though he was petrified of being on stage. Over the next few years, Stephen became a hairdresser, owning his own business which he ran for many years.

He did demonstrations at Spiritualist Churches around the area, but Stephen was keen to get through to people who didn't know anything about Spiritualism. He booked himself in at Morley Town Hall, for an evening of clairvoyance. He was billed as "Yorkshire's youngest medium". Even though there were only about 40 people at the event, he realised he'd enjoyed himself – it went very well. This was the start of Stephen's 30 years-and-counting career, of performing to the public at events around the country and beyond.

Eventually, Stephen gave up his hairdressing business to concentrate fully on his clairvoyant psychic medium performances, and all the admin and travelling that goes with booking a couple of hundred performances a year.

What are Stephen's personal beliefs?

Stephen doesn't believe in reincarnation. When spirits talk to him, he passes the messages on, although he doesn't know what the message means. When he's on stage, his spirit guides and inspirers are stood with him. He does believe in God, although he has no clear vision of who or what God is.

Regarding ghosts, Stephen has encountered one once. A friend of his rang Stephen in the middle of the night, very agitated, asking Stephen to come over because he had a ghost in his living room. Very reluctantly, Stephen got dressed and drove over to his friend a few miles away. When he got there, he could see his friend and girlfriend were petrified, so they all sat on the settee and waited to see if the ghost would appear to Stephen. After just five minutes, the ghost did materialise, walking out of the wall, across the room, to stand by the fireplace. It was wearing old-fashioned clothes and it was not see-through, but looked solid. Suddenly it grabbed Stephen's leg, and he nearly jumped out of his skin. Then the ghost disappeared. It wasn't evil, but it certainly wasn't nice. It was totally different to a spirit which is friendly – this definitely was not friendly!

Hopefully you will understand a little better who this incredible man, Stephen Holbrook, really is. He's the nicest, friendliest, human being you could ever hope to meet. He is so accommodating, ever keen to help, got a great sense of humour and real human empathy. He understands what we go through when we lose someone special.

But lo and behold! We haven't really lost that person – it turns out that they are there, just one message away from us. My goodness, Stephen is the link that connects us to that much missed family member on the other side.

With Roger's amazing testimony and visual proof of life after death, and Stephen's amazing messages from people we thought had ceased to exist, we now know with absolute certainty that life goes on. The physical body has been buried or cremated, but who needs a physical body when there is eternal life to continue living? We will all join our friends and relatives in due course, but in the meantime, they are with us, even in the same room as us, and that is such a comfort that will help us get through the next few years, until we meet them again.

In the accompanying video to this chapter, watch what we filmed at one of Stephen's shows on the SLS camera – Roger is there, pointing at Stephen's books, as Caroline said, "This was totally in keeping with Dad's love of books and education." There are other spirits there too, but we can't say who they all are.

The second part of the video is the audio of Stephen's reading, when my mum came through. It's so emotional for me, but so wonderful at the same time.

To see where Stephen is performing, or to buy his books, look at his website:

www.steveholbrook.co.uk

Chapter 8

The Society for Psychical Research, Aaron Lomas Investigates Roger

It's been a long and complicated road getting Roger investigated by any scientific organisation. Initially, when Roger first started showing up on the equipment that I got, specifically the SLS camera, I was so amazed, but I didn't know which scientist or organisation it would be best to contact.

I had already read three of Rupert Sheldrake's books. I knew he was a very highly regarded biologist and author with some views and theories outside of the norm, compared to other Western scientists. The first book I read was *The Presence of The Past/Morphic Resonance and the Habits of Nature*. The second was *Dogs That Know When Their Owners Are Coming Home*. The third was *The Sense of Being Stared At*. All three of these books were absolutely fascinating, and Rupert Sheldrake is a very famous and highly regarded person within his specialism of investigating psychic and telepathic events. He has designed and carried out very extensive scientific studies that prove telepathy and other so-called supernatural abilities, which are actually inherent in humans and animals. He has a theory which various others also subscribe to, that we are surrounded by Morphogenetic Fields (Morphic Fields), which allow us to transfer thoughts over infinite distance, and this is the mechanism by which telepathy actually operates.

Other scientists have replicated his tests, proving that they are accurate and valid. His view of the brain is that it is a receiving and transmitting device, similar to a radio, which tunes in to the electromagnetic waves which surround us. The brain tunes in to these Morphic Fields, and it is through these electromagnetic fields that thoughts are transmitted to any creature of the same species, as well as creatures of other species. We don't have our own memories locked in our own brains; scientists have never yet been able to locate any memories within our brains. This theory certainly seems to me the most plausible explanation – it hasn't been disproved. The fact that dogs can anticipate when their owner is coming home has been proven to be real, and not just dogs – cats and many other species of pet also have proved beyond doubt that this is a genuine, well-documented ability. We have even experienced it with our own dog, and I'm certain many readers will have had similar experiences.

I contacted Rupert Sheldrake and told him about all the amazing activities of Roger since he died – he was fascinated, but he told me that Roger's activities in the afterlife are not an area that he is actively researching, so he was unsure exactly what it was I wanted him to do for me. I asked Rupert if he was able to put me in touch with any other scientists who are actively researching Roger's types of activity, which I suppose would be defined as supernatural, or maybe paranormal.

He responded with a very helpful email, telling me that the Society for Psychical Research has a long-standing interest in paranormal events, and he would copy my message to Dr Callum Cooper at the University of Northampton, who was a member of the SPR Spontaneous Cases Committee, in the hope that he could point me towards someone who might be able to help me in my enquiry. He agreed that it did seem too good an opportunity to waste.

I wasn't familiar at all with the SPR, or indeed any scientific organisations studying paranormal occurrences. When I read about them, I found that:

> The Society is the first organisation to conduct scholarly research into human experiences that challenged contemporary scientific models. The Society was set up in London in 1882, the first organisation ever to examine

> claims of psychic and paranormal phenomena. They hold no corporate view about their existence or meaning – rather their purpose is to gather information and foster understanding through research and education. Their members represent a variety of academic and professional interests all over the world and they welcome active researchers and volunteer helpers and also those who wish to learn about the subject. They publish quarterly a scientific journal which has been published continuously since 1882 containing reports of new research, book reviews, and correspondence, copies of proceedings describing occasional in-depth research, and have a library that's open to the public, and members may borrow books by visiting in person or by post.

I told Ali Mather that I was trying to get some scientific opinion on Roger's activities, as I felt that the book I was writing about Roger would be severely lacking if I didn't have an input from some respected scientific body, or people in the paranormal field, to give their views on Roger's and Joan's activities. Ali told me not to worry about getting the SPR onboard – it wasn't important. She recommended that if I did want any input of this kind, then the Arthur Findlay College would be worth approaching. This organisation is "the world's foremost college for the advancement of spiritualism and psychic sciences". I did approach them and got in touch with a very helpful lady there who was a medium and a teacher of mediums. She was familiar with all the electronic equipment I was using, and she was very positive, but in the end, many months later, we were never able to meet up, so I never got any active involvement from them.

On Rupert Sheldrake's recommendation I contacted Dr Callum Cooper at Northampton University, and he thanked me for doing so. He told me to email Dr Graham Kidd, who was the Chair of the Spontaneous Cases Committee of the SPR, and he said he would circulate my details and videos about Roger to the Committee, and get back to me with the best possible way forward.

I contacted Dr Graham Kidd, Case Coordinator at the Spontaneous Cases Committee, part of the Society for Psychical Research. My first email didn't get a response, so I sent a second, and he replied, apologising that my first email seemed to have slipped through the net. He said that the SPR were very interested in what I was telling them about Roger, and the Spontaneous Cases Committee would discuss Roger's case at their meeting the next week. He couldn't find my YouTube links to the videos, so he asked if I could attach them along with any other video I had, so that they could examine them. I sent him the links and all the other information.

Eventually I got a reply from Dr Graham Kidd, telling me that Aaron Lomas, a member of the SCC and a PhD student in parapsychology was keen to take on Roger's case, and he would be in touch. Graham told me that the SCC usually work in pairs, so he has asked if anyone else would be available to come up to investigate Roger. He thanked me for getting in touch, and said, "Here's hoping Roger stays in touch for a while longer." This was in response to me saying that I felt time was of the essence, as I was worried that at any time Roger might stop showing up on camera, as I had been led to believe that spirits such as Roger only stay around on Earth communicating for a year or so, then gradually stop communicating. I was so worried that if Roger were to do this, then we would lose our golden opportunity of investigating him scientifically, when he was clearly so keen to help the scientific community investigate and assess him in any way they wanted. Roger was evidently very keen to further human knowledge of life after death, and everything connected with it, as I was. He did seem to be so keen to pass on his new-found knowledge to all of us here on Earth, and I was fully aware what a unique opportunity Roger was giving us all, and it would be utterly tragic if it was wasted by any needless delays.

A while later I got another message from Dr Graham Kidd, in which he told me that another experienced member of the SCC had also expressed an interest in investigating Roger.

I received an email from Aaron Lomas telling me he had been sent the case notes about Roger, and he had watched the videos I had sent the Committee. He was looking into the various items of equipment I was using and wanted to know more about them. He said he was willing to come up with this other experienced member, who was copied in on the email, for a possible interview about the case presented and to find out if anything else had occurred previously, or after the videos were made.

I thanked Aaron for his very positive reply and sent him details of all the equipment I was using, and all of Roger's appearances on camera. I told him Roger showed up every time I turned the camera on, and I was very hopeful that if he could come up to visit us at home, Roger would show up on camera, and we hopefully would get a video of Aaron, his colleague and Roger together. I suggested some dates which would work for us, then left it with him to find out when he and his colleague could come and visit.

He responded, saying his colleague was very busy at the moment, so might not be able to visit us to investigate Roger. Aaron explained that unfortunately, due to the Committee's policy and procedures, he wouldn't be able to come and visit us by himself, but he had asked any other members of the SCC if they were willing to join him to further investigate this case. He said he knew of a couple of members who were interested, and hopefully he'd hear back from them soon, if they were not currently busy with other cases they were undertaking.

A week or two later I had another email from Aaron, in which he said that unfortunately no other Spontaneous Cases Committee members were available in the near future to come and investigate with him. He said that if no one else could come up with him to do the investigation officially, then he was thinking he might come up by himself, if he didn't hear anything by the Committee's next meeting in a couple of weeks' time. Then he would plan to come up to meet us for a couple of days, to have time to fully investigate, and catch up on whatever else had occurred. I still don't fully understand the Committee's rules, as Dr Graham Kidd had implied that investigations can be carried out by an individual, just that they usually work in pairs. I really didn't mind one way or the other whether the investigation was carried out by an individual or a pair of investigators. The most important thing to me was that *someone* should investigate Roger's case.

This is indeed what happened in the end: Aaron came up to visit us at home by himself, so his investigation was done in a personal capacity, not as an official investigation of the Spontaneous Cases Committee of the Society for Psychical Research. I was totally happy with this as I could see that Aaron had tried everything he could to get a colleague to come with him to investigate Roger, but it was more important that the investigation was done as soon as possible, as otherwise, the way things looked to me, the investigation might never happen at all. I was totally confident from everything Aaron told me in his messages that he would investigate Roger in a thoroughly scientific manner which was totally in keeping with the procedures and principles that the Society for Psychical Research adhered to. I really didn't mind whether there were two investigators or one – I was just so pleased how keen Aaron was on this case, and I was very confident that he would find evidence to confirm scientifically what I already knew – that Roger was indeed visiting us and showing up on the SLS camera as a spirit.

I am so incredibly grateful to Aaron, that he somehow sensed something important and special in everything I had told the SPR about Roger's revelations on camera. Aaron had exactly the same information as all his colleagues at the SPR, but for some reason only Aaron could see just how special Roger's case potentially was. This really could be the most significant case the Society for Psychical Research might ever get in its 140-plus years of history, the case which might come the closest to finally proving, once and for all, that there really is an afterlife – and Roger was trying to show the Society the definitive proof – but only Aaron was giving Roger the attention that he deserved.

In June 2023, Aaron came up for a couple of days to visit us at home and to experience first-hand Roger's appearances on the SLS camera, his communication through the Ovilus talking dictionary, and his flashing of the lights on the K2 EMF meter.

Meeting Aaron in person for the first time, Caroline and I were both very impressed with what a pleasant and friendly person he was. His messages over the preceding months were very polite and friendly and in person he was just the same. I had wondered if people in this scientific field might be, how can I put this politely? – maybe a bit weird, a bit strange – but there was none of that about Aaron.

When he arrived at our house and started his investigation, I was very impressed with just how thorough he was. He wrote copious notes on every little detail about where we lived, the room we were in, the equipment in the room, the furniture. I don't know what he wrote, but I could tell that he was very meticulous in everything he did. It was very reassuring to know that he was evidently following his training in researching this case, to report back to his colleagues on the Spontaneous Cases Committee of the SPR. I knew that whatever he said, it would be scientifically credible. If he were to agree with us that Roger indeed was showing up to us in spirit form, then this would give the scientific stamp of approval to our assertion to the world, that here was proof, on camera, of the afterlife. Of course, there was a long way to go to get to that stage, and there were plenty of opportunities for the proof to fall short in convincing him and his colleagues on the committee.

Aaron asked me how I did my investigations into Roger, so I showed him the setup I used whereby I filmed everything I did on my smartphone, while all the equipment was visible on screen. I knew that I had my equipment, in theory, too close together for the readings to not be affecting adjacent equipment, but I explained that I did this so that I could have a record on video of all the readings the various bits of equipment gave, and I saved every video I made. Every time I turned on the SLS camera, I recorded it so no event on camera would ever be lost.

Aaron used my K2 meter to take background EMF readings in the rooms where we filmed with the SLS camera. It became apparent that the way I investigated and filmed what I believed was Roger's spirit was not in line with how inherently sceptical scientists would approach this, but I felt justified that what I was doing was totally valid. I could tell when the K2 meter was being triggered by an adjacent piece of equipment, or when it was being triggered by something else, namely Roger's spirit, when he was deliberately making the K2 respond in order to emphasise some point or other.

The way Roger triggers the K2 meter is not in the same way that spirits on ghost hunting programmes apparently do it. On TV programmes, and what all conventional ghost hunters do, is to take background EMF readings in a room. In areas where the EMF reading is higher than elsewhere, that is where they believe a spirit might be present. The higher the reading, the closer the spirit. I have always noticed that this isn't the way Roger operates. Is Roger different to other spirits, or is the conventional well-accepted premise wrong? I'm not sure what the answer is. I do know that the way Roger does it is as follows: When the K2 meter is very close to Roger, the reading is just the same as if he wasn't there at all. When he wants to, he can make the K2 meter display a high reading, normally as a short flash or burst of higher-than-normal EMF. He might flash it slightly, maybe half full scale, or he might flash it very strongly, right into the red (full scale). He might flash it once, or maybe many times.

Roger only seems to make the meter flash at all when he wants it to – he uses it more as a way to converse with us, or at least to emphasise a point that I or someone else is making, as in an ordinary conversation between two people – if someone is talking, and the other wants to agree with them, they might just say yes, every so often, or they might show a thumbs-up gesture, or they might nod their head. Obviously, all these conventional physical options are not available to Roger, so what he does is to activate the electrical K2 meter, as it's something he is able to do. It wouldn't make sense to constantly emit a high electric field all the time, as that would just be wasting energy. It would be like a person walking in the bright sunshine with a torch turned on – what's the point? It just wastes the batteries and serves no purpose whatsoever. However, that person might use their torch in bright sunshine to signal to someone in the distance, by flashing the torch – that would be a very useful way to use the electrical energy within those batteries. This is definitely how Roger operates, and I suspect how all spirits operate – it's just that investigators haven't previously had the chance to test a willing spirit before. This is the ground-breaking opportunity Roger is offering Humankind – the chance to test him, scientifically, with whatever tests they can think of. Will any spirit ever make such a generous offer again? Maybe not.

Aaron did recommend a couple of textbooks that I should read about scientific paranormal investigations, describing how to take background readings etc., before starting an investigation. I did get these books later, but to be honest I found them of little help for me. Many times, I would turn on the SLS camera to try and chat with Roger, and most times he would show up within a few minutes, but sometimes it could be quite a while before he showed. I knew that if I were having to document on paper every little detail about background EMF levels, and many other parameters such as temperature, air pressure, humidity etc., I would rapidly get overwhelmed with all the paperwork and I wouldn't have the SLS camera on as much, and there would be a danger that I would actually miss any appearance by Roger. I felt that Roger was probably of the same view as me – he would probably stop showing up due to impatience with me writing all these notes prior to actually talking to and filming him. So, I carried on doing things my way after Aaron had done his investigations over the couple of days that he was with us. I do fully appreciate that Aaron was following his scientific training to the letter, and his colleagues at the SPR would expect him to do so, so it was important for a credible Spontaneous Cases Committee report to have followed these well-accepted procedures. Hats off to Aaron, but in the real afterlife world that Roger was showing me, red tape and excessive paperwork was definitely a hindrance – I just needed to get on with it and actually do it, if I were not to miss the very glimpses of the afterlife Roger was allowing me to see.

The first part of the video for this chapter is footage taken by me as Aaron sits on the settee in our living room, taking notes about Roger's case. I am just starting to turn on all my equipment, but the Ovilus is already on, and on the screen, the Ovilus has the word *report*. I say to Aaron, "You're writing a report, aren't you?" and he confirms that he is. As I lift up the SLS camera and start looking around the room to see if Roger is visible on it, instantly I see Roger is there, and he's on the settee next to Aaron, as well as another spirit who I think is the spirit of Poppy, our late and much missed spaniel. Roger shows the word *beside* on the Ovilus, and I'm just amazed, because Roger *is* beside Aaron on the settee, as Aaron writes his report. What could be more impressive than that? Roger, I knew, was keen to help the scientists to investigate him. And here he is, right next to the scientist who is investigating him, and he is actually there beside him on the settee, and he is saying absolutely the most relevant words possible through the Ovilus. Well done, Roger! I knew you would do this if you could. So, I tell Aaron what I'm seeing on camera and invite him to come up and see Roger on the SLS camera, which he does.

While Aaron is looking at the screen of the SLS camera, Roger is in front of the big dresser behind the settee, and Aaron is talking about the fact that the SLS camera could be creating a stick figure because it is picking up on the features of the dresser. I say to Aaron that the SLS camera is having to deal with so much information which it processes, in order to conclude there is something there, and when it does, it puts a stick figure on the various shapes and features within the wood of the dresser. Roger says *appear* on the Ovilus, and then the word *talking*, and I acknowledge that he has appeared to us, and we *are* talking.

I tell Roger that we're going to go through into the kitchen with the camera, to see if he will come with us and show up there. I tell Roger we need good proof for Aaron, so Roger says the word *possible* on the Ovilus. I tell Roger that we need some top-quality material from him, so that when Aaron writes his report, he can convince his colleagues that this really is you, Roger, showing on the camera.

When we get into the kitchen, I can see Roger is there, but initially it's hard to be sure. So, I ask if he can get in front of the white cabinet, which is where he was in a previous video when he appeared to his daughter Alison on camera, which he confirmed by using the word a*lley*, as he always called her Ali. This had been exactly the right word for him to use, as there was no *Alison* in the Ovilus database, or anything else suitable – only the word *alley* was remotely appropriate.

Roger is in front of the white cabinet briefly, but then he disappears, and Aaron talks about the various shapes and features of the cabinet which could trigger the camera, so we continue to look for Roger's spirit in the vicinity. While looking for his spirit, the camera puts a stick figure onto Caroline, and

I explain to Aaron how the SLS camera was designed to put stick figures onto living humans, but also how, when a person is more than 12 feet away from the camera, it can't see them, and so it doesn't put a stick figure on them. This is just inherent in the design of the camera, and our tests have proved this to be the case. As Caroline comes within 12 feet of the camera, she gets a stick figure placed on her. Very soon we see Roger's stick figure in front of the white cabinet. This stick figure disappears, and the word *deplete* shows on the Ovilus. This could be Roger explaining why we are having trouble seeing him on camera – maybe his energy is depleting. This is a common problem with spirits according to all the programmes I have seen, where their energy does deplete, and it can stop them from giving us the various signs that they can sometimes give us.

After a couple of minutes, Roger does show up again, above the dog's bed on the floor, and gradually he gets taller, and moves slightly, so he is in front of the white cabinet again. The Ovilus says the word *self,* which maybe is confirmation that it is him when I am talking to Aaron, saying I think it's Roger. All the time this is going on, Aaron is using the K2 meter, checking for EMF levels in the vicinity.

As we talk to each other, I keep asking Roger to come out with some convincing words on the Ovilus, to prove to Aaron that it's really him. He comes out with the word *thing*. I'm not sure if that is convincing or not – probably not. He comes out with the word *supper* when he is by the cooker, so that's quite a suitable word. He comes out with the word *hug,* which he often does when he's talking to us, which I think is him saying he is giving us a hug or would like to give us a hug. He comes out with the word *observe,* which is appropriate, as we are observing him. Or maybe it's him observing us. At this point I think Roger is in front of Caroline, as although it looks like a stick figure on Caroline, which is how this SLS camera is designed to work, the stick figure doesn't line up well with Caroline's body, and to me it looks like another stick figure in front of, but not connected to, Caroline.

Roger says *wave* on the Ovilus, and he does appear to be waving. After a little while, I ask Caroline to walk slowly towards the television, which she does, in the hope this stick figure in front of her will separate from her, and then it does. As she walks back again, the stick figure stays near the television, and then near the white cabinet, and the Ovilus says *grandmother*. I ask if he is referring to Joan, or if it's Caroline he's referring to, as Caroline is a grandmother. Spirits always seem to come out with slightly indirect or cryptic words, so it is a case of interpreting what they are saying, to some extent. Roger has never said the words *yes* and *no* in response to questions, and I have noticed on ghost hunting programmes this is usually the case. When I say to Roger, "That definitely is you, isn't it, Roger?" when I'm sure it is, he says the word *fact* on the Ovilus. I explain to Aaron that he often says *fact* when he is confirming something that I have said – similar in meaning to the word, *yes*. Now he says *door* on the Ovilus, while he is by the door of the cabinet. He then says the word *night*. I don't know how relevant that is – I don't understand.

His stick figure gets a lot lower, and I am not sure what is happening, then suddenly there's another stick figure over the dog's bed, so I ask him who that is. He comes out with the word *men*. I keep pressing Roger to tell us who this other spirit is – he says the word *paranormal*, and then he comes out with a few other words, which I don't really understand, like *tight*, and *wide*. I say to Roger that Aaron is waiting for some really good words to prove it's really him – he's waited months for this day to come, and Roger needs to come up with something very special for Aaron – not that I'm putting any pressure on him (I am really!), but we do need him to do something really impressive. He comes out with the word *board*. Ever since this video was taken, I didn't know why he said *board*.

I thought this was a very random, unspecific word, but then, just a few days ago while writing this chapter, I realised that this is a really accurate word, and I just hadn't appreciated it – until now. Roger is low down, in a very low pose, and he is right next to the skirting-board – so *board* couldn't be a more appropriate word for him to use. A year on, and I have only just seen the significance of the word that he has used. If I find this frustrating sometimes – Roger not using the best word – then just think how frustrating it is for Roger when I am not understanding a very good word that he is giving me. Sorry, Roger, for being so slow on the uptake. It's quite awkward, this physical human/spirit communication, when all we've got is some clunky technology which although incredibly impressive, is probably not easy for the spirits to use, but it is the best of what we've got. It's probably a bit like two humans trying to talk to each other when they don't speak the same language, and they are fumbling to give each other basic signs to make themselves understood. Although occasionally they do make themselves understood when it's something simple to convey, anything slightly more complex becomes virtually impossible. No wonder the spirits and us get equally frustrated at times. I must give Roger all due credit for his valiant perseverance in trying to get his message across to us, even when we can't always see it or understand it properly.

It's this communication problem that highlights exactly why I have been so keen to get mediums involved with Roger, as when they are good, they are able to relay some very accurate messages from the spirits.

After I dismiss Roger's word *board* by saying to him, "I don't understand it. It's not very special. What else can you come out with?" he then says *water* – I can see that that is a totally relevant word, as he is above the dog's water bowl. All the while this has been going on, the second spirit is still visible over the dog's bed, and I still don't know who it is. As Aaron and I talk about this other stick figure, I say that I did think it could be Poppy. I explain that the camera is only looking for human shapes, so even with the spirit of a dog, if the camera spots that there is something there, it would superimpose a human-shaped stick figure onto it, even if that spirit is not human-shaped. Actually, all spirits might not be human-shaped. They could well be a simpler shape than a human. I have read that human spirits don't have legs. Maybe they don't have arms either. Maybe it is just a general shape that is an elongated cloud of energy. Maybe dog spirits are the same shape as human spirits – no one knows this for sure as far as I'm aware.

So, no more of note happened on camera during Aaron's visit. The plan was that eventually he would write his report, relay it to his colleagues, and then I would get to see that report. I did appreciate that Aaron was very busy with his PhD work and other things, so I realised that this report might not be ready for some time.

Just a few weeks after Aaron's visit to us, he had some terrible news – his dad had died. It's always a great shock to anyone, even if you might have been expecting it. I was very sorry for Aaron, and I didn't push him at all with anything relating to Roger's case. I said I fully understood that he would be grieving and wouldn't have the time or the inclination to do any of his academic work for the time being, so I obviously wouldn't expect any progress on the report about Roger. When he felt up to it, hopefully in a few months' time, maybe we could have discussions on any more things we could do to investigate Roger.

Aaron was very appreciative that I wasn't going to pressure him at all. I had always told him that my aim was to write about the Society for Psychical Research, and the Spontaneous Cases Committee in particular. I fully understood that everything he had found when he visited us to investigate Roger was on a personal basis, as his colleagues were too busy, or otherwise unavailable, to join him for an official SCC investigation.

Several months later Aaron was back in touch, and he explained that he was resuming his PhD work. I gently pressed him to see what more we could do together in order to further investigate Roger. He had said previously that he was wanting to get his own SLS camera, to experiment with it and to fully understand it, and to do a whole battery of tests on it. As I had one spare, I told him I would send it to him, to keep, in order that he could start looking at it and see what it could do and start doing his various experiments and assessments on it.

Aaron received the SLS camera and pretty soon embarked on his initial assessment of it. I don't know all the details, and I didn't need to know, but Aaron had planned a programme of tests that he would put the camera through to evaluate it, and to write his ever-meticulous reports on it. He used it in conjunction with his laptop computer, and he immediately proved that it worked, insofar as seeing living human beings was concerned. I was so intrigued to know whether he might see any spirits on his camera, so in our communications I kept asking him if he had witnessed any discarnate spirits on camera. Each time I asked him he had nothing supernatural to report to me, but he was steadily working his way through his many tests on the camera, as his spare time allowed, which from the sound of it wasn't very often. I couldn't help but wonder whether his own dad's spirit might show up to Aaron on camera, but he never did. I also wondered whether Roger would show to Aaron on his SLS camera, so I sent him a photograph of Roger, as photographs are well-known to be trigger objects for spirits. Trigger objects in general do help spirits to come through in some form, as I had found out when my own mother came through at a Stephen Holbrook show. I had her Order of Service in my pocket, my dad's jacket on, and my mum's pen in my pocket. The very first question Stephen Holbrook asked was, "Has anyone here tonight got an Order of Service on them?" I was the only one in the audience who had, and sure enough, it was my mum who came through with a brilliant, accurate, message for me. This was recounted in great detail in the earlier Stephen Holbrook chapter.

I asked Aaron to speak to Roger and have the photograph to hand when he had his SLS camera on, just in case Roger was inclined to show up for him. But as far as I know, he never did show. Because Aaron was also busy with his PhD work and other things, I was very conscious that Aaron's long list of tests for the SLS camera was very time consuming, particularly with all the detailed notes that he was writing for his report.

I kept asking what tests he was aiming at with the camera, once he was familiar with its operation. What would it take for him, as a sceptical scientific paranormal investigator, to be persuaded that the SLS camera was indeed seeing a real spirit, and not just creating a stick figure when objects in the picture could be fooling it into believing there was something there when there wasn't really? Aaron told me that he was planning to do various tests with the SLS camera in a neutral room, where the walls were very plain and featureless, painted in a light colour. He told me that he might be able to do it at the offices of the Society for Psychical Research in London, or possibly at the University of Northampton where he was doing his PhD.

Being well aware of the book I was writing about Roger and the fact I was going to write about the SPR and Aaron in particular, I suggested that I would like to come down and meet him for some SLS camera testing wherever he wanted to carry it out. He explained that it wouldn't really work very well in his own house, and maybe the SPR headquarters weren't the most suitable, so probably Northampton University would be the best place to try it out. In a few weeks' time the Easter holidays would be upon us, and as my job comes with school holidays (that's one of the main attractions of my part-time job as a school bus driver), I suggested to Aaron that if I came down over the Easter holidays, whichever day suited him, and we tried out the SLS cameras at the University, that could work very well. He agreed this was a good plan, so he said he would look into it and book a room on a day that was convenient. He suggested Good Friday – that was fine with me, so he booked the room and it was all systems go to see what, if anything, we would find on the two SLS cameras.

Every time I have put my SLS camera on at home and spoken to Roger, I had told him about the plans with Aaron, which he obviously knew anyway. Roger was very keen to do this scientific testing, and I was very optimistic that Roger would do something impressive. The University was about 120 miles from my house, so as always, one basic thing that always impressed me would be Roger's ability to show up anywhere. Although this is a very basic ability of a spirit, I am still amazed that they can do this, just go wherever they like, seemingly just by thinking about it.

When Good Friday came around, I set off with a few hours to spare so I didn't have to rush down, although I knew the traffic would probably be a lot lighter than normal, it being a bank holiday. I got to the University half an hour early and met Aaron in the car park. He had a little bit of difficulty getting in, as there was virtually no one on campus, but eventually he managed to speak to someone in an office, via a phone, and they were able to let us into the building so we could go to the room that Aaron had booked for the day.

When we got to the room, we both unpacked our own equipment, and started setting up to do some assessments of the SLS cameras. Aaron had a number of tests planned, with his camera and mine viewing simultaneously one part of the room, in order to see whether both cameras would pick up the same things. Before we got to that stage, I told Aaron I was going to just try and see if Roger might show while I searched with the SLS camera, looking for his spirit on the plain white walls of the room. Aaron was making his copious notes about everything, and while he was sat at the table writing his notes, I started exploring the room, searching for Roger's spirit.

The second part of the video for this chapter shows everything that happened next.

I had been hoping Roger might show very quickly, but as time went on, I realised he was not in the mood for showing up instantly today. I was actually starting to worry that maybe I had been too optimistic. Maybe this was a test too far for Roger. It was approaching almost 14 minutes before finally I saw something on camera, a couple of fleeting glimpses of a spirit visible just for a couple of seconds in total.

Because it was so hard to get Roger on camera, I restarted the SLS camera and tablet computer, just in case they were misbehaving – they are normally so reliable.

Thirty-two minutes from the start, Roger finally showed properly while I was filming Aaron through the SLS camera. Aaron was stood at the table with his notebook in hand, and I could see a stick figure on Aaron, although it wasn't the full size of Aaron, so I wasn't sure if this was Roger in front of him or if this was Aaron's own stick figure. I kept asking Roger if he would do something to prove he was there. I looked away from Aaron with the SLS camera, to the plain white wall to the side of him. Then all of a sudden, I saw Roger on the plain white wall. Bingo!

I congratulated Roger on showing up, and said, "Well done!" I told Aaron I was going to keep filming while Roger was showing. I didn't want to do anything that might stop him from showing, so I told Aaron that Roger was right next to him, and asked Aaron to stay where he was while I filmed and I would show him the footage shortly. As I kept talking to Roger, saying how fantastic it was that he had shown, and well done, how I had known he would show, Roger kept briefly flashing the K2 meter to acknowledge what I was saying.

As I talked to Roger some more, I explained that I had reset the SLS camera earlier when I wasn't seeing him, as even though I didn't think the camera needed it, I thought I better try doing it, just in case the camera was not seeing him for some technical reason. Roger kept flashing the K2 meter – he was obviously empathising with my dilemma and agreeing with my sentiments.

I ask Aaron to sit down in his chair, and Aaron asks exactly where Roger is. He holds out his hand gently and says, "Is he here?" And I say, "Yes, Roger is just by where your hand is pointing." Aaron sits down and I ask him if there's anything else he needs me to do while Roger is showing on camera, in order to prove that this is Roger in spirit form, showing on the SLS camera. Aaron says, "No, that's fine." I'm still trying to get Roger to use some very appropriate word on the Ovilus, to doubly confirm that's him on camera. He has already said *wave*, which is something he often says on the Ovilus when he's around – it does look like he is waving, but whether he is literally waving to the camera or not, obviously we can't be sure. I tell Aaron that everything we are filming at this moment is going to be incredible proof when the book is finally published, and everything I write about the experiments today, and the SPR in general, is going to be such an amazing part of Roger's story for people to read in the book. I explain to Aaron that there is the word *Rodger* in the Ovilus, but it is spelt R O D G E R, whereas Roger's name doesn't have a D in it. If Roger could say *Rodger* on the Ovilus, that would be fantastic extra proof. So, I ask Roger to do this, but he never does.

So, after appearing continuously on the plain white wall next to Aaron for just over 4 minutes, Roger suddenly stops showing on the SLS camera. A minute or so later I see Roger showing up on camera, but in front of the desk where Aaron is sitting. In this position, Roger looks shorter than previously, but he is in front of all sorts of bits and pieces which could be thought to be triggering the camera, seeing what isn't really there. I knew it was Roger in this new position in the room, but he didn't come back onto the plain white background as before. I kept talking to Roger while Aaron kept writing his notes while sitting at the desk, with Roger in front of him. Eventually, after 44 minutes of video, I told Roger I was going to turn the equipment off and stop filming, as he had done everything we needed him to do, and there was nothing more he needed to prove. After a break, I will turn the camera on again, and we will then embark on all the two-camera testing that Aaron has got planned.

We did an extensive range of tests with the two SLS cameras simultaneously filming the same position in the room, to see whether the cameras would see the same thing. Even though the cameras were side-by-side on the table, looking at the same point several feet away, inevitably, each camera did have a slightly different view. Maybe for this reason, sometimes one camera would see a spirit and the other wouldn't, and vice versa. I'm sure this spirit that the cameras continued to see was Roger, and he was helping us with our tests, but I was so elated from what Roger had done on the plain white wall that I was just following Aaron's instructions on autopilot, while we did all the tests he wanted and he made his copious notes of the results. We did a whole series of tests, such as where one of us would be physically in shot of the cameras, while the spirit was also in shot with us, and we would slowly reach for the door to the room, then open or shut it, to see whether the spirit would change positions, while it grew smaller under our arm, next to our body, and at what point it stopped showing.

Aaron was able to comprehend the reasons of how and why spirits behaved the way they did on camera, but I was not really listening, so I didn't take in everything Aaron was telling me. He did explain how the camera has a lot of settings which can be altered, and it can show some very clever three-dimensional views of an object in a room, and the viewpoint on the camera can be altered to move around this three-dimensional object, and a whole series of measurements can be taken. It just shows how unbelievably complex and clever these cameras are – they really are packed with software and features which makes them so much more than mere entertainment devices, which is what they were originally designed to be. I have never adjusted the settings on my camera – I have always just used it as it came out of the box – I've never felt the inclination to change it, as it works so well as it is. For something available so cheaply (as little as £20 or less, unused in its unopened box), it is incredible just how sophisticated they are. They were obviously never intended to look for invisible spirits, but what an amazing incidental ability it turns out they have, which was purely an accidental feature never intended by the clever boffins who designed the SLS camera in the first place. The camera does work in conjunction with some equally impressive and complex software on a computer – in my case, on the tablet computer. It just goes to show how this sophistication can be employed to great effect to prove life after death, which is exactly what we have just done!

After several hours of fascinating testing on an empty university campus in the UK, in a very plain white room, I believe that we may have proved beyond any doubt that SLS cameras really can see spirits, no matter what any super sceptic might tell you. The fact they weren't designed to do this doesn't take anything away from their incredible ability to actually do it. They really can see the spirit of someone who one year ago was a physical human being, living on this Earth. He was my father-in-law. Now he is my discarnate father-in-law, and he is here with us, showing up in his spirit form on an SLS camera, proving to us, the scientist and the enthusiast, and you the reader, that this is really him. He is real, and he is giving us the most valuable message possible, a priceless lesson for anyone willing to listen and to read his story which I think would sound something like this:

This is Roger, previously a total sceptic, and I'm here on camera, and I'm showing you that I still live, but now I live in the afterlife.

This is where you will join me in the future, and who knows exactly when that will be? But at some point in time, you will join me and Joan, and all the rest of your family who have gone before you. This is my message to you, and as a lifelong educator, who trained as a teacher after graduating in English at Oxford University, and as a lifelong book aficionado and enthusiast, I am telling you that here I am, and this is your future that you are looking at on camera. You are free to make of this revelation whatever you want to make of it, but a top scientist has just helped prove to you that I am real. This SLS camera really is looking at my spirit, after my earthly body had given up the ghost. I wish you all the best in coming to terms with this totally unprecedented message that I'm giving you, and I look forward to meeting you on this side, whenever your time comes. I urge you to make the most of your new-found knowledge – it will change how you live the rest of your earthly physical life. If I had known what I now know, I would have done things differently, but I am now able to give you that certain knowledge which I doubted.

To get in touch with Aaron Lomas, contact him on Aaron.Lomas@northampton.ac.uk

Chapter 9

Liz Murphy, Amazing US Medium

We first got in touch with Liz Murphy over a year ago. Or, more accurately, I should say Liz Murphy got in touch with Caroline. It was really a most bizarre way that Liz got in touch in the first place. Caroline has been a keen knitter for many years, following in her mother's footsteps. Caroline had signed up through an email list for a free knitting pattern from Liz when she had her Resilient Knitter website.

Out of the blue, Caroline got an email from Liz in which she said:

> Liz here! Just in case you're wondering how I got your email, at some point you signed up for one of my free knitting patterns via **Resilient Knitter. But since then, I quit knitting.**
>
> *Why?* Because a few years ago my sister-in-law passed from cancer at the age of 39.
>
> She was only a year younger than me and it ***shook me to the core.***
>
> *Her death and my grief sparked a spiritual journey, and in the process I realized I'm a medium.*
>
> *What's that mean?? I have the ability to communicate with your loved ones in spirit and provide detailed evidence that life continues on after the physical body is gone.*
>
> *I know.* ***As a self-proclaimed atheist, my whole life, it still sounds crazy to me too.*** *But it's true.*
>
> *And as I've developed my skills over the last two years, this ability has been incredibly* ***healing*** *not only for myself and our family, but it's brought so much* ***comfort*** *and* ***peace*** *to hundreds of other clients I've worked with as well.*

Now, if mediumship isn't for you, I get it.

And you're welcome to ***unsubscribe*** *at the bottom of the page.*

But if you've experienced a profound loss and you're longing to connect with your loved one in spirit, I'm offering ***5 FREE mediumship readings*** *– in exchange for completing a short feedback form of your experience.*

Here's how it works:

Reply to this email (first come first served!)

I'll send you a link to my scheduling calendar, so you can choose a day and time that works best for you.

We'll meet online via Zoom for your appointment.

What others have said about their mediumship reading with me:

It was great talking with you today and I am still smiling from what you brought thru. You're making a wonderful difference in people's lives! – Kim

You gave me so much comfort. Thank you! – Joy

You brought me so much peace today – Suprita

If you made it this far, thank you for having an open heart and mind.

And if you're ready to learn how connecting to your loved ones in spirit can make coping with grief easier, check out my website or you can find me on Tiktok@mediumlizmurphy

Warmly,

Liz Murphy

Mediumlizmurphy.com

p.s. Know anyone else who may benefit from a FREE mediumship reading? Feel free to forward this email to them.

Caroline told me about this offer to have a free reading with this new medium, who was a knitter. She was very keen to take up this offer, but I really felt Liz Murphy couldn't be much of a medium if she had suddenly switched from knitting to mediumship. It just sounded weird in the extreme. What on earth could she do that was real and genuine? (This was me being narrow-minded.)

We talked about it on and off for a couple of weeks, then Caroline said she would go ahead and try it out, just in case. This was about three months after we had the fantastic reading through Ali Mather at her home, near where we live. Amongst other things, I wondered, could a medium who's halfway round the world really connect with Joan's and Roger's spirits, when we are living in the UK, the medium is in the US, and who knows exactly where Joan and Roger reside?

So, Caroline went ahead and booked the reading with Liz Murphy. Although I did try to persuade her to tell Liz Murphy that I would be filming in our living room using the SLS camera, while Caroline was on her iPad on the Zoom call with Liz, Caroline was frightened of scaring Liz off if she were to tell her exactly what our plans were – so we didn't tell Liz what we were doing. We would just do it anyway, because there was a great chance that nothing much would happen at all, so there would be no explanation needed, and we would have tried it, and it would have failed.

When the appointment came around, I turned on the SLS camera well in advance of the appointment time, just to see if Joan and Roger were there on camera. Maybe they would be keen to try out this experiment with us.

Caroline connected to Liz using a Zoom link, and the call started. Roger did show up on our equipment a few minutes before the reading started, and then again about four minutes after the reading had started. From this point on, Roger was there on camera in our living room for most of the time, but he couldn't be seen on camera for a few minutes at a time here and there. While he was on camera, he was sometimes in the green chair where he often puts himself, and then other times he was above the settee, next to Caroline.

Liz brought through some pretty accurate messages from Roger, but it sometimes was hard work for her to get to the truth from the pictures that Roger evidently was giving Liz. Some of the messages could be a bit confusing, but once Caroline clarified a few things, the messages were very good. *In retrospect, looking at the reading, many times I feel that maybe Roger's communication with Liz was slightly difficult for Liz, and this was down to Roger, not down to Liz. Certainly, some of Roger's messages were spot on, but some weren't.

*** A note from Liz**: *I want to clarify that spirit is* ALWAYS *accurate. They never need to learn how to communicate with us, nor is it ever difficult for them to do so. I greatly appreciate Jeremy and Caroline for their patience and support in letting me practice while I was learning mediumship, however, if there's any difficulty in the communication, it is* ALWAYS *the medium that gets it wrong. Communicating with spirit is a little like playing charades, and when I got it wrong, it's because I was interpreting something incorrectly.*

Over half an hour into the reading, Liz invited Caroline to ask any questions that she might have, whether Caroline wanted her to contact anyone else? Caroline said she would love to hear how her mum, Joan, was doing, as she doesn't hear much from her these days.

Liz connected with Joan almost straight away. Joan was obviously better at giving some good pictorial messages to Liz than Roger, as what Liz relayed were incredibly accurate messages from Joan. One message Joan gave to Liz was a picture of Joan with lots of children. She asked Caroline if there were lots of siblings. Initially, Caroline said no, obviously thinking this wasn't an accurate message. Then suddenly she realised the picture Liz was getting from Joan was from her work as a nursery nurse, where she was surrounded by lots of young children. This was the job Joan had done for many years, and she thoroughly loved it. Liz continued to relay incredibly accurate messages from Joan, saying how Joan was very loving and easy-going, although she could keep control of all these children by just saying the right things. She was firm but fair. Liz thought it was a gift – not just anyone could do that.

Other messages were that Joan had lots of time for everyone – she would happily talk to anyone, such as members of the family. She ran the household very efficiently, making breakfast every day for everyone, before she herself left for work. She had incredible patience, great kindness.

Liz asked Caroline if Joan had sisters (she didn't) – it felt like she had two sisters, maybe very close friends. Joan did have two very close friends, who she had from a very young age, until she died.

Joan told Caroline what a good job she did of looking after Roger – thanks for taking care of him, he could be a handful. Caroline did a better job of it than she could do herself.

"Could your dad have been a little bit gruff, the way he talked to people?"

"Yes."

"She was more patient than maybe he deserved sometimes?"

"Spot on!"

"Her own passing was very sudden?" that was totally correct. "She knew of an underlying problem, a heart issue?" Caroline confirmed this.

"They loved each other very, very much."

The bright flowers Liz talked about, "They must attract butterflies – if you do see one, think of your mum."

At this point, Roger is still showing on the SLS camera, and very briefly, Joan appears just behind and above Caroline for a few seconds. After a couple of minutes, Roger stops showing on the SLS camera, then doesn't reappear for a few minutes.

"Would you describe him as being selfish?"

"Yes."

"All these things he's told me are all about him, it's him and you, I don't see anyone else around."

"The gravestone, it's all about him."

Caroline tells Liz a story about the gravestone, how initially it was not right, he had organised it, but it was awful, then he realised it wasn't right. She then organised a new one.

"It was almost just a name" – Liz.

"Yes, it was *just a name*" – Caroline.

While Caroline is telling Liz about the gravestone, Roger has been showing up on the SLS camera in the green chair, and then Joan reappears above and behind Caroline again, and she is there for about a minute while Roger remains in the green chair. Then Joan disappears again.

At this point it is nearly the end of the reading. Our time has run out. So, Liz and Caroline wrap things up and say goodbye. It has been a phenomenal reading from Liz. Joan's messages have been so accurate, more accurate than Roger's, but again, it does seem to be that Joan has given Liz the most accurate pictures in her mind. Maybe Roger's pictures have been more ambiguous and confusing.

I contact Liz Murphy via email to compliment her on how fantastic the reading was with Caroline and tell her what we were doing with the SLS camera, and *why* we were doing it. I explain to Liz the whole business of Joan and Roger giving us signs, then how we got the electronic equipment to try and track Roger down, which we did very successfully. I asked Liz if she would let us talk about her and her amazing mediumship reading in a book I'm writing about Joan and Roger, and if she would allow me to use the video for people to view.

She responds really politely but says that although our project is fascinating, this type of experiment isn't how she works as an evidential medium. She is certain that there are mediums out there who do work in that capacity, and she wishes us all the luck finding one, someone who is just the right fit for us.

I contact her again, thanking her once again for everything she did for us, and trying again to see if she would relent on her decision. She thanks us for our understanding, says we are welcome to write about the experience, but she would appreciate it if we didn't include her name in the video or the book. I'm very disappointed, but I fully understand her reasons. I always realised that not being straight with her at the beginning was a mistake, but when we went ahead and filmed without telling her, I wasn't expecting anything positive to actually happen during the reading – my expectations were very low. ***How wrong I was!*** I felt so awful that we had been dishonest with Liz, but on the other hand, she might well have not proceeded if we had been upfront at the start, and then we would never have known what could have happened.

Several months after this fantastic reading from Liz I discovered a very famous US medium, whose name I can't reveal. I was convinced that her story would be the final concluding chapter of this book, and her reading would be fantastic, and I would write about how great she was, and the cachet of a famous name would really help with publicity for this book. After reading her books, I also thought she would be fascinated with Roger's story, how he shows up on the SLS camera, especially how he showed during her reading with Caroline in our living room, in the UK.

Unfortunately, when her reading finally happened, it was very, very disappointing. It was a very expensive lesson for me – I believe that the message for me from the spirits was: *Don't be fooled by someone who promotes themselves so much and charges a fortune for her readings. Mediums who do showbiz probably won't necessarily be doing it for the right reasons.***

I totally got what I deserved.

** **A note from Liz**: *While some mediums aren't ethical and don't do it for the right reasons, most do. And just like in every profession,* *even mediums have off days. We're working with energy, so if we're not feeling well or our own energy is off for whatever reason, the reading may not work properly. However, it's the medium's responsibility to handle that situation in a professional manner. If a paid reading doesn't go well, then the medium should take responsibility for their work and reschedule for another day or give a full refund.*

More than one year on from Liz Murphy's excellent reading, having turned things over in my mind for a few days after the anonymous medium's reading, I decided I had nothing to lose in contacting Liz Murphy again, to see if one year on she might relent, and help us to try again with a reading, but this time I'd be totally honest and open with her.

I emailed her a message, almost pleading with her to let us do another reading as before, while filming with the SLS camera in our living room, but this time asking Joan and Roger some different questions, to try and get answers to some more existential questions.

Liz didn't reply straightaway. In fact, as the weeks went on, I was convinced she wasn't going to reply to me at all. I really was upset, but I fully understood her position.

Six weeks after I sent her a message she did reply.

Hi Jeremy,

Thanks for reaching out, it's so nice to hear you're still working on your book. Creative projects always seem to take on a mind of their own, don't they? You never know where they'll end up!

Gosh, I'm sorry you had such a disappointing experience with the anonymous medium. I have heard of her and I've also read that complaint from so many clients of famous mediums in general.

I really enjoyed reading for Caroline and would be happy to read for her again.

Warmly,
Liz

I was so over the moon to get this positive reply, so I booked the reading with her straightaway, but I was not 100% sure if she was giving me permission to write about her in the book, and to use the video, freely using her name. Just to clarify, to avoid any misunderstanding on my part, I sent her a message spelling out what I was hoping to do, to write about her openly and use the video without taking her name out – was she okay with this?

She replied that she was totally fine with me using her name in the chapter and in the video, and she was looking forward very much to seeing the chapter once I had written it. I was finally starting to see how the spirit world works, that what we plan doesn't always go how we imagine it will. Sometimes the complete opposite seems to happen, but eventually if we give it time and plenty of thought, we will realise why things have turned out this way. I could tell that I had been given an important lesson; and I was more than happy to learn from it. The anonymous medium was a lot less than they were cracked up to be, and I should trust my own instincts, going with people who I felt comfortable with, not people who got themselves the best publicity, whatever their methods to achieve that publicity. The old adage, *you get what you pay for*, doesn't really apply here. In fact, the opposite seems to be true.

When the day came for the new reading with Liz, we soon realised there had been some sort of mix-up, somehow, with the start time for the reading – something to do with trying to work out what the equivalent English time was, converting it to American central time – we had to abandon the session.*** While we were attempting it, we were able to see Joan and Roger on the SLS camera in our living room for quite a bit of the time, but they weren't there constantly. They had evidently shown up, just in case it went ahead.

*** **A note from Liz:** *You don't need a medium for spirit to be with you. As a medium, I'm not calling them in from somewhere else. They're always right there with you and part of your life.*

A week later we tried again, and this time the session worked perfectly from the start, just apart from the SLS camera being a bit temperamental initially. I restarted it, and then all was fine. This was a bit of a surprise, as generally the camera is very, very reliable. This time Joan and Roger were in the living room waiting for Liz, and they never disappeared from view for the whole of the session while Liz was connected online. The whole time they were by Caroline, in front of the settee where Caroline was sitting – they were obviously really keen to make the session a success. It was actually a bit of a surprise that Joan was there all the time, as with the session a year ago she had only shown up for about a minute altogether. Maybe Joan was getting the taste for communication with Caroline via a superb medium.

After saying hello, Caroline told Liz about the butterflies that we had seen as we left Joan and Roger's cemetery a few months prior. In her previous reading, Liz had told Caroline to look out for butterflies, signs from Joan. This particular occasion, as we left the cemetery after tending their grave, we were talking about signs. We had been watching a programme about signs from spirits, including butterflies, and Caroline was asking her mum whether she would give us a sign. At that moment, suddenly Caroline noticed many butterflies on two or three gravestones, and as we looked, we saw more butterflies in the bush and the tree nearby. It could have been 30 butterflies, all the same type – red admirals. And, also, there was a robin singing in the tree. Caroline also told Liz that she had her butterfly earrings in this evening, while the reading was happening.

I had a list of questions prepared for Caroline to ask Liz, but Caroline didn't read them out verbatim – she approached them in a roundabout way. The first question to Liz was:

Can she ask spirits questions and get answers from them? Liz said "definitely". Caroline asked how she sees spirits, and Liz explained that she sees them in her mind. She has seen spirits that look like people, but that is not generally the case. They tend to give Liz pictures in her mind, to convey the message, using references they're trying to get across. For instance, if they show her a person with grey hair and wrinkles, that's telling her to convey that they're elderly. For her, that is someone over 80.

"Do you see them as they were when they left us, or in their prime?"

"Both, usually as they were when they passed, but sometimes in a specific time period."

Caroline tells Liz that she's got a list of questions that I had written for her, so she introduces me to Liz, and I say hello, telling her I'm on the other side of the room, filming on the SLS camera, and so far, Joan and Roger have been sat there by Caroline as the session proceeds.

Caroline asks Liz the next question by initially talking about signs that Joan gave us after she died, and how when we told Roger about this, he was more or less completely disinterested, didn't believe at all in an afterlife – how does he feel now?

Liz says that Roger is giving her a sign of a turtle, as if to say "slow and steady wins the race".****

**** **A note from Liz:** *Even though we were asking Roger questions that couldn't be validated, Roger gave me this evidence to let Caroline and Jeremy know that it was in fact him I was connected to.*

It reminds her of when her own grandad passed, she had had big disagreements with him about the afterlife but after he died, he came through to Liz with the message that "the afterlife is not how I thought it was, but it's not how you thought it was either". Liz says that at this time she was an atheist. The spirits have this greater perspective "yes, he definitely concedes that it's not how he thought it was". Caroline says that she saw a turtle for sale today in a shop, not a real one, but a toy one, so she's thinking she'll have to go back and buy it. Liz confirms that Roger did give Caroline that sign.

Caroline struggles to ask the next question, so I ask it of Liz, which is "can Roger remember everything after he died. I know he was aware that Caroline was there as he died. Can he remember everything from then, onwards. And that's another thing: Where is he?" Liz says it depends on your belief system. But the way she sees it, it's instantaneous: "It's like waking up from a dream. One minute you're here, the next minute you're here (somewhere else). It's such a relief, losing your physical body. It's like getting home at the end of a day and taking your shoes off. For us, it's like taking our bra off," Caroline laughs and says she did wonder if that's what she meant. "It's effortless, no pain, no discomfort. No physical body anymore, so no eating, sleeping, no playing golf anymore. As they don't have physical eyes any longer, they don't see things in the way we do. They just sense it. They are just aware of it."

"How does Dad feel about Jeremy writing this book. Is he happy the way he's doing it?" Liz says there's no right or wrong way to do it. Before this reading, Liz was preparing for it ahead of time, and Joan and Roger were letting her know for us to remember that Spirit is all around us. They are there all the time. They're omnipresent. We don't have to specifically ask them things – they're there, wherever we go. It's just a matter of us moving our awareness to them. In our physical life we're limited by time and space. It's not for them; they can be everywhere at once. Roger's so excited, especially for me and my spiritual awareness. Roger says to me, "In the beginning it was a bit of a stretch for me (Jeremy), but now I am feeling more comfortable with it."

Caroline asks me if I agree with that, and I say that over the years we've had lots of relatives and friends die, but it was only after Joan died that we got the signs, and then, when Roger died, he took over, and we love these signs, and since then we are really enjoying this communication with them, with the equipment that we got after Roger died, and it's been like a constant dialogue – and it's been fantastic.

Caroline asks Liz if her mum and dad hang out with other relatives. Liz says, "Yes, absolutely, we're all connected, each and every soul, this physical life does create a stronger connection."

Liz quickly adds one more thing that Roger has just told her, that he's so pleased for me, he can see how much peace and comfort this whole business has brought me, and he's happy for me. It's brought enrichment and enhancement to my life. Writing the book has helped me to get that.

Caroline asks Liz if they are aware of reincarnation, and she says, "Yes, they are aware of their previous lives. It's like a Rubik's cube where each little square is another life that's been lived – they're all different aspects of our soul, just another piece."

Caroline asks Liz another question, about signs that Joan and Roger give, particularly where they turn on our television, or similar electronic devices. In fact, Caroline tells Liz that our TV did turn on last night while we were deeply asleep, around midnight, so again, we feel that's a sign from Joan, or was it Roger? And Caroline explains to Liz that our TV has an extra remote-control switch to stop it turning on – it used to turn on more easily. This extra remote switch was put in to try and stop some of the signs which, although we do love them, we were getting them so frequently it was stopping us sleeping enough.

Liz explains that because we use electronic equipment to communicate with them, we are comfortable with it, particularly the K2 meter which is to detect electric fields (EMF), the Ovilus, which is a talking dictionary which Roger uses, and also the SLS camera, which is a camera which can see the spirits by superimposing a stick figure on the picture where it sees or detects the energy of the spirit, as seen in the videos. Caroline tells Liz we have lights and lamps that turn on as well and asks, "Is it just their energy which does this, as they don't flick a switch, do they?"

"Yes, absolutely."

"And how do they give butterflies as a sign?"

"There's two ways of doing this – I can't prove it, but butterflies and birds have electrical navigation abilities in their brain, so the spirit could influence them. Also, the butterflies could be there anyway, and the spirit manages to get your attention, to make you notice it."

"In your experience, have you had spirits move things around physically?"

"Yes, we've had lots, but about 15 years ago my husband and I had a spinning wheel that my grandfather had built me, and while we were lying in bed, it suddenly pivoted out from the wall and I thought it was one of my three boys under our bed, playing a prank on us, which he often did. When I looked under the bed, there was no one there. So, it wasn't children playing pranks, it was my grandad moving the spinning wheel out from the wall. We had various toys that moved. We had toys with lights on, but this one was one of those toys you actually had to wind up, to make it go forward, like a little truck – we had that go across the floor by itself."

"And you think that was spirits trying to get your attention?"

"At that time, I was a little bit scared. I didn't really understand what's going on. I knew it was something, I just didn't know what it was. Now I know it was nothing to be afraid of, just Spirit trying to get my attention."

Caroline says, "Jeremy has got a question for you."

"Hi, Liz, I'll stay on this side of the room, because I'm still filming, because Joan and Roger are still here showing up on the camera as spirits"—Caroline turns the iPad round so I can see Liz—"If you could just give a very, very brief potted history of your abilities, and what made you become a medium. You said you were an atheist, but could you see ghosts?"

"I grew up in a very religious family. I've always been able to hear, see and feel things. For instance, when I was 12, I woke up one morning, I knew my great-grandmother was sick, but this morning I was brushing my teeth, and I just knew she had died. I came down to breakfast. My parents said, 'Your great grandma Ella's died.' 'Yes, I know.' What I had in those days was mostly feeling. You know you feel someone is standing behind – you turnaround and there was nobody there – it was a lot of unknown things. I didn't know how I knew. But I knew.

"As I got older, say my late 20s, we were in this house, and things were happening. There are some things going on here which were really obvious, we couldn't explain away. We'd been on vacation. We came back to the house. We had a baby, and we had one of those electronic play tables where you press a button and it plays things, music, or whatever. We open the front door, and it started talking, and it says 'it's good to have you home again'. **It doesn't say that!**"

"So, when did you decide to do this, as a business effectively, and what made you decide to do that?"

"I think it was 2019. My sister-in-law had passed. She was a friend from middle school. In fact, it was through her that I met my husband. She passed to cancer, and she was 39, and it really set me on this healing journey. If this can happen to her, how do I want to live the rest of my life? So I started doing all this personal inner work, and doing that, other things came into my awareness. I call it *following the breadcrumbs*. Spirit nudging me in directions. There was one night, I was lying in bed, watching a movie on Netflix on my phone, and it was the strangest thing. It was like there was another movie playing in front of the movie on my phone, and it was my grandfather who had died a year before – it was this one who I had had an argument with about religion, and it was him and two of my great aunts, and they were just sort of peeking round the corner. It was as if they were not wanting to startle me, but they wanted to have a conversation with me, and it was at that moment that I realized I wasn't just an observer of Spirit – I could actually talk and have a conversation with them. And, of course, my brain is going, *what the hell is going on*? – and I started doing a little more research, and a little more research, and I found out that what was going on was actually called *mediumship*, and it was nothing to be afraid of – it was just our loved ones wanting to communicate with us. And so, once I started working with people, it had such a profound effect on me. I could see what a healing impact it had for others, and it became almost this obsession. I really needed to do more and learn more, and I don't know if you've had that, but it just feels like it's something you have to do, and it's just become part of who I am now – part of what I have to do – and I love it, if it can help other people."

"Do you believe in God now?"

"That's the interesting thing – I still don't, but I believe in a *oneness*, but I'm open to experiences and ideas, thoughts from other people, learning from others. If I can validate it, I will believe it. And so far, I've been shown this beautiful oneness, and if I had to call it God, then I guess that's what it is. All our souls are connected, and I guess it's all of our souls that are connected together that creates some kind of energetic power, that oneness, which I guess you could define as God.

"It doesn't really matter what we believe in. If we want there to be a God, then there is a God. It's so deep – it's so hard to explain, but I believe we can create our own spiritual reality."

At this point, I told Liz that we were at the end of our time, and I thanked her so much for such an amazing session. Caroline also thanked her, then we said our goodbyes.

I've been studying these videos – the one from a year ago, and the one from a week ago – they're so absolutely fascinating. There are many things that I can deduce, I think, from what I'm seeing of Joan and Roger on camera, and the messages that Liz is getting from both of them. A year ago, Roger was on camera for most of the session while Liz was talking, but he wasn't there for all of it. Joan was only there on camera for a minute or two.

A year later, both Joan and Roger were there on camera before the session started, as soon as I turned on the SLS camera, and they stayed there, continuously visible near Caroline, for the whole of the session. As Caroline says to Liz at one point, her mum, Joan, wasn't into all this sort of thing. So, one year on, Joan, I feel, has realised just what a useful thing it is, to be able to relay messages through a medium, allowing her to actually communicate in whole sentences, with her daughter Caroline. Joan and Roger wouldn't hang around if they didn't want to be there. Their personalities and characters in life are exactly the same now as they were, now that they are spirits in the afterlife. If Joan didn't want to do something, she wouldn't. And one year ago, she probably didn't know what this mediumship business was all about, or at least, how positive it could be.

The messages that Liz got from Joan and Roger one year ago are impressive. Although Roger's messages were a lot less impressive than Joan's, in studying these videos, I think I realise why Roger's messages weren't as good as they could have been – Liz picks up on the point that in every picture that Roger gives to Liz in her mind, it's always Roger does this, Roger does that – there is normally no one else in the picture. It's all him, and Liz does pick up on this, saying to Caroline, "Would you say he was selfish?" and she agrees, "He was."

On the other hand, Joan's messages were incredibly accurate, totally spot on in virtually every little detail. In fact, they were so good it occasionally threw Caroline. She initially didn't always realise the message her mum was giving her through her pictures in Liz's mind. For instance, when Liz asks Caroline, "Were there lots of siblings?" Caroline says *no,* and suddenly realises all the little children around Joan are the children at the nursery school where she worked. Joan's messages via pictures to Liz were obviously more accurate than Roger's and included a lot more detail of other people involved. This was how Joan was on Earth; she would include others when she was talking, "*We* did this, *we* did that," whereas Roger would say, "*I* did this, *I* did that."

It's so incredible to be able to see Joan's and Roger's personalities as clear as day in Liz's incredibly accurate messages. Any ambiguity or uncertainty with Roger's messages is purely down to Roger not giving Liz an accurate view of events, whereas Joan's accuracy enables Liz to give such an impressive and accurate summary of her life here on Earth.

This whole exercise with Liz has been so enjoyable, and although we got off to a shaky start with Liz one year ago, it's obvious to me that we were destined to get back to Liz, in order to get the most incredible messages from Joan and Roger. The anonymous medium really did me a massive favour in a way, by being such a disappointment, but it did take me a little while to understand what the lesson was that I was being given, and to see the path I needed to take.

Liz has been so gracious in all her messages to me and has proved beyond any doubt that she was the one destined to conclude my final chunk of research for this book. She has tied up all the loose ends that I had in Joan and Roger's story. She has knitted all the pieces together (excuse the pun), to conclude their out-of-this-world, but true, account of their life together in the afterlife. This chapter has proved to be such an important lesson for me, and I hope also to everyone who reads this book and watches the video.

The video for this chapter, as with all the videos for this book, is long – it is the longest of them all. Initially I had wanted to keep them short, but I rapidly realised that to make them short would be to discard the majority of the footage, which is all so informative and instructive for anyone who has been inspired to read Joan and Roger's story.

To any of the Smartphone Generation who don't have the stamina to study the long videos, just skip through them, or just watch the five-minute video for Chapter 1– but to everyone else, I thoroughly recommend you watch the whole video when you have the time, as I know you will be amazed. The latter part of the video for this chapter shows Liz telling us about her own journey on becoming a medium, which is so fascinating and revealing. To anyone who feels they want to try and do this for themselves, Liz's example would be the greatest inspiration.

As with all of the chapters in this book which have a video, to watch, simply use your smart phone on the QR code on the front cover to access my channel on YouTube: **Joan and Roger Alive In the Afterlife**, the same as the title of this book. Alternatively, the URL link below will access the YouTube channel if you are accessing it using your PC.

https://www.youtube.com/@joanandrogerafterlife/videos

To get in touch with Liz Murphy simply go to https://mediumlizmurphy.com

Chapter 10

What Joan and Roger Have Taught Us

Just what have Joan and Roger taught us? Well, I hardly know where to begin, it's all so momentous, everything they have shown us.

Well, if we start at the beginning, Roger and Joan have appeared to us on camera as spirits in the afterlife. Until Joan started giving us all her signs after she died, we didn't know for certain if there was an afterlife at all. So, after all the funerals we went to over the years of family and friends, we didn't know whether life just finished abruptly and beyond that point a person ceased to exist. Joan was the first person to prove to us that she did still exist after she had died.

Joan's proof was an amazing start to this whole chain of events – we knew from her signs that there really was an afterlife, but total-sceptic Roger was still adamant there wasn't and wouldn't even talk about Joan's signs with us. It took Roger to die himself before he would realise that he had been so wrong – there genuinely was life after death. Roger then carried on doing what Joan had initiated – he eagerly showed us his spirit on camera.

We now knew with absolute certainty that there was life after death, because we could see with our own eyes, spirits on camera. Of course, all the sceptics will say the camera isn't really seeing spirits at all, it is merely an electronic device being fooled into thinking there's a spirit there, when in reality it is just the electronics misbehaving, tricking itself into seeing something that isn't really there at all. How could we possibly prove that the sceptics were wrong, that these were real spirits on camera? Well, this is where my mission to get scientific validation of these spirits comes in.

I have been desperate from the very start of this investigation to get respected scientists to confirm that what the camera was showing was indeed a real spirit. This is where the Society for Psychical Research comes into the story. After pressing the Society, which is the oldest organisation in the world that was set up with the specific aim of proving life after death, finally I was able to get one of their paranormal investigators to look into the case of Roger.

Luckily for me, even though the Society's long-time member, the Chairman of the Spontaneous Cases Committee, didn't seem overly enthusiastic about what Roger was showing us on camera, Committee member Aaron Lomas must have sensed there was something intriguing about Roger's case, and was inspired to investigate. When he came to our house and I showed him what I thought was Roger on camera, he wasn't totally convinced – being a trained sceptic, he couldn't be sure if the so-called *spirits* on camera, the green stick figures, were genuine spiritual energy, or whether or not they were just the camera being confused by what was in shot. Even though Roger was talking through the Ovilus, using some very appropriate and relevant words sometimes, this wasn't enough to convince Aaron, but he did seem to be open to persuasion – if Roger could just provide further, better proof.

About a year later I went down to meet him at Northampton University where he was studying for his PhD in parapsychology, where we could do some more in-depth tests with the SLS camera. This was a perfect place to do such tests, as we were able to use a plain and almost featureless room that wouldn't confuse the camera. We did get 100% proof on camera that the green stick figure was indeed a spirit. There was no way the camera was being tricked by what it was looking at, as it was viewing a totally plain and featureless white wall, and there, showing up in front of the wall, was the green stick figure that was Roger's spirit. Aaron was happy that we had done everything necessary to prove this was a real spirit – the camera wasn't being confused by the features in the room. This was the complete and totally unambiguous proof I had been so desperate to get – confirmation from a respected and sceptical scientist – this was definitely a spirit that the SLS camera was detecting! I knew this was Roger on camera, even though he wasn't able to say anything totally unambiguous on the Ovilus to announce to the world that it was him, but that didn't matter. He kept showing on camera for over 4 minutes against the plain and featureless white wall next to Aaron.

One important thing to bear in mind with the green stick figure on the SLS camera, is that the camera's interpretation of the spirit's poise and deportment shouldn't be taken too literally. What looks like Roger's limbs, the position of them and any apparent movement of them, probably isn't actual and accurate – spirits apparently don't have limbs – so the camera is just struggling to interpret what it is sensing, but it genuinely is sensing *something*. The one million infrared dots are being displaced by the spirit's energy field, and the camera knows for certain something is there, so it places a stick figure where it thinks this energy actually is.

Imagine the SLS camera image as being like an Air Traffic Control radar screen, which we've all seen on TV, where the radar is detecting the aircraft, so it places a symbol on the computer screen for the air traffic controller to see exactly where the plane is, in order to be able to keep track of it. We don't see a photographic image of the actual plane detected, that's not necessary, but we do see where that plane is. Well, this is what the SLS camera is doing. It's not a lifelike representation of a spirit's shape and limb position, but it is a representation of the approximate size of the spirit's energy field, the amorphous fuzzy shaped energy field that comprises it.

We now have the most eminent organisation in the world which looks into possible proof of life after death, confirming that we had got 100% genuine proof on camera of life after death. There was nothing more Roger needed to do – he had done it. He had proved to us and to the world that he really is there showing up on camera, after his physical body had died. He, of all people, the person who didn't believe there was anything after we die, was there showing us he is still alive, showing us he had been wrong – we really do live on after we die.

How do we know that this spirit was Roger, and not just a random spirit off the street? Well, even if it was a random spirit who happened to be passing while we were filming with the camera, that is still 100% proof of a real spirit on camera, but I knew it was Roger. Several mediums have confirmed that this is Roger. Liz Murphy, in particular, has come through with some very accurate messages from both Joan and Roger while we were seeing spirits on camera. For her to be coming out with such accurate messages, especially the accurate messages from Joan while her spirit is showing up on camera, that essentially proves that the spirit we are seeing on camera is the spirit giving the messages.

Over the past couple of years, I have become very slightly psychically aware, as apparently anyone can – it's just a matter of practice, and of trusting your instincts. From the demeanour of the spirits on camera, I can tell it's Roger and Joan, while their messages are being relayed to us by a medium. Roger has a pattern of behaviour that is uniquely him – he tends to appear in particular places in the room, and normally looks bigger, whereas Joan appears in other locations, normally, and looks a bit smaller. Also, at the start of this SLS camera adventure, Joan hardly ever showed, but Roger would show a lot. This is exactly how their personalities are, how they were when physical people on Earth as we knew them – Joan would not want to do this, she would get bored and go away to another room, whereas Roger would be so keen to try it out, he would be persistent and keep trying. After some time getting used to being a spirit, Joan is now showing up a lot more often. I'm certain she now appreciates that an excellent medium can relay her messages to us, so she is now more than happy to stick around while we all try.

This proof on camera of life after death has initiated a huge quest by me to find out everything I can, in books and TV programmes, to see what insight I can glean into the whole afterlife. I was recommended a book that I had never heard of, *Journey of Souls*, by Michael Newton. Michael Newton is a hypnotherapist, and over many years under hypnosis, dozens of his patients have all relayed how they had had previous lives prior to their current physical life on Earth. He has documented all the evidence from all his patients over many, many sessions, and they all have essentially the same story of what happens when we die and become a spirit, then are reborn as a new human on Earth. While someone is under hypnosis they cannot lie, but they can access their very deep-seated memories, which are normally inaccessible whilst conscious. Past life memories are very deep-seated and normally inaccessible in our day-to-day existence. This very compelling evidence confirms that there is reincarnation, that we live our life on Earth, we die and our spirit goes into the afterlife, then some years later our spirit is reborn into a newborn physical person on Earth.

After reading this book it became apparent that there are many books written by many authors, who all have this same story – the same version of what happens when we die and get reborn. All these books by all these experts in their field corroborate the concept of reincarnation. The medium Ali Mather proved to my complete satisfaction that our son, Patrick, had indeed had a past life which he was no longer aware of, but as a small child he used to talk about a lot. He had been a sailor on a sailing boat. Ali Mather's Past Life Regression therapy on Patrick had him confirming this to be the case. It is very widely accepted that young children can remember their previous past life, but as they get a bit older, maybe six or seven years of age, these memories disappear, and the child can no longer recall that past life.

Just a few weeks ago before I finished writing this book (with Roger's help and direction, of course), I read an amazing book by a great author. *Our Eternal Existence*, by David Gaggin, is the most impressive book I have read in the last few years relating to the subject of life after death. David Gaggin is an engineer/scientist, who for many years worked for The Boeing Company, the aircraft manufacturer. He was in charge of cockpit design, avionics and flight systems. This was in the days when Boeing made the most reliable and dependable aircraft. After leaving Boeing, David worked for NASA amongst other organisations and then set up his own microwave defence company which employed 3500 people at the time of his retirement. Throughout his life David had wondered what happens when we die, and he spent a lifetime researching and reading up everything available, from every source possible – from ancient writings through to contemporary books like Michael Newton's *Journey of Souls*. From all of this vast research, he was able to filter the information to get to the truth of what the afterlife is all about – in fact, what *everything* is all about, including our universe and all other universes. He describes his book as a *metaphysical perspective of reality*.

The fact that David Gaggin is a totally down-to-earth person from a conventional Western background, striving for answers to his own questions, gives his book all the more credibility. As such an impressive individual who has proven over a lifetime to be such a discriminating judge of the reliability of the information he is researching, then his conclusions are surely totally dependable. What he says, I think, can be relied upon to be the most accurate explanation possible, for everything.

His explanation of reincarnation is that we as humans continually reincarnate, over millions of years, so we do have literally thousands of different lifetimes, both on planet Earth and other planets elsewhere, even beyond this universe that we currently inhabit. It is very hard to comprehend the magnitude of exactly what life is when you read an explanation like this.

All the books I've read explain life and reincarnation as the process of our eternal souls being educated. The purpose of life is to learn from your mistakes in a physical lifetime, so that the next time we are reincarnated into physical form we will be a better spirit. Over countless lifetimes our spirit gains more knowledge and becomes a higher level being, or consciousness. Our spirits are all a part of a wider collective consciousness. It is this consciousness which creates physical realities – conventional Western science has got it wrong – matter doesn't conjure consciousness, consciousness creates matter! And we are all connected as a tiny part of this greater consciousness. Another way of phrasing it is that this all-powerful consciousness is God. The old idea that an all-powerful God is aware of everything we do turns out to actually be true.

Another book that I found very insightful is called *Beyond Photography,* by Katie Hall and John Pickering. It is about their encounters with orbs, angels and mysterious light forms. It's nearly 20 years old and recounts how when taking photographs on their digital camera, they noticed some strange light anomalies. The more photographs they took, the more anomalies they would see on film. They didn't have any explanation for this initially, but after a lot of investigating, they concluded that these orbs and other light anomalies were intelligent forms showing on the camera. They did all sorts of experiments to rule out the possibility that these were just camera malfunctions, or reflections within the camera of stray light in the field of view. All the photographs were black and white, and many of them are published in the book. Technology has inevitably been transformed over the last 20 years, so a lot of the photographs aren't of the highest quality, and being black and white it's hard sometimes to appreciate the enormity of what we are seeing. Some of the light anomalies appear to be little winged creatures, which they describe as *fairies*. These have an uncanny resemblance to some of the light anomalies we saw on our cameras, which did look like miniature winged creatures of some form. If nothing else, this book supports the idea that many of our light anomalies on camera were the same type of light anomalies being photographed by other people, which tends to confirm that our light anomalies were genuine paranormal or supernatural events and not just our cameras malfunctioning.

The most inspirational and thought-provoking TV programme that I've seen is *Paranormal Caught on Camera*. This programme, so far, has seven series, and comprises clips from all around the world of various paranormal or supernatural events, such as: ghosts on CCTV cameras; strange, other-worldly beings such as Bigfoot and UFOs. The sheer breadth of video footage does tend to confirm that there is so much that we humans just don't understand. Each video clip is dissected by a range of experts giving their opinions on what we are looking at. The majority of clips are obviously completely genuine, and I would watch some of these completely jaw-dropping videos at a total loss as to how to make sense of what I was looking at.

The very first episode I saw was one that Caroline recorded for me, before I had ever heard of the programme. In this episode there was CCTV footage from a school in Dublin, Ireland. When the school is empty at night, and there are no people in the building, some metal filing cabinets and lockers in the corridor start moving by themselves – rocking backwards and forwards, apparently without anything making them move. It's totally baffling, but some while later I saw an interview with the school headmaster, and apparently the school was built on some ancient burial grounds, so it's been built over many old graves. It would seem that the spirits of some long-deceased people move the metal lockers. The whole concept of poltergeists, spirits who move physical objects, is borne out by this video footage.

As a child I didn't want to think about ghosts and everything related, because I was so scared of things like this. But as an adult, I now realise that all of these spooky things are actually real, they really do exist. So, in my lifetime I have come full circle courtesy of Joan and Roger. They have proved to me on camera that what I suspected as a child is real. There really are such things as spirits.

Maybe the biggest lesson of all as David Gaggin and others explain, is that we think of ourselves as physical beings who eventually die. We need to think differently, we've got things back to front. We are actually spiritual beings, who every one or two hundred years or thereabouts, get incarnated into a physical body here on Earth – or maybe on another planet. The purpose of this physical life is for our spirit to learn whatever lessons they can while in physical form. Learning lessons while being a physical entity is the quickest way to learn all the lessons that we need to learn, and this is the very essence of why we live our physical lives in the first place – it is our spirit's classroom, where we can have our period of accelerated learning, before we return to our natural spiritual home, before we once again return for another physical life learning experience. And so, it goes on…

I'm still not exactly sure of the difference between the soul and the spirit – they seem to be very closely connected, and some people use the terms interchangeably. It's certainly the case that, as souls, we get reborn as physical beings repeatedly with other souls who we know. These *soul groups* tend to stay together every time they get reincarnated. This means that Caroline and I, our spirits or souls, know each other from previous lives. We always felt we were soulmates and almost certainly we are. It also means that probably Joan and Roger are souls who we've lived with before in physical lives here on Earth. And it's not just Joan and Roger, of course. It's probably a lot, if not most, of our family – we've all been around the block together many times before.

The reason we don't remember our past lives except when we are young children, is so that we take our physical life here on Earth very seriously. If we could remember that we had lived before as a physical person then it might reduce our ability to learn the lessons from the current physical life we are leading, and God's plan is that we learn these lessons as well as we can. If we fail to learn our lessons in a lifetime, then it means that we will come back again in another physical life, to try and successfully learn the particular lessons we were trying to learn this time. It's always in our own interest to learn our life lessons as effectively as we can, so that eventually we become a higher-level spirit.

So, I mention God – who is this God person, or thing? Another name for it is Universal Consciousness. I'll quote David Gaggin's definition: "A mind consisting of a single system of thought made up of an infinite number of individual units of consciousness or spirits all working towards a single goal of perfect understanding while embracing the guiding emotional principle of pure love toward all beings, i.e. God."

Some people don't believe in God. When I was a teenager and stopped believing in the Catholic faith, I was wrestling with where everything came from, including life, how the universe and beyond worked. I still believed in *a* God, but maybe not the conventional religious definition of God. So, I suppose I was believing in a Universal Consciousness. I really couldn't subscribe to the Western scientists' view that the whole universe came into being with the Big Bang, by some incredible accident, and that there had been nothing there beforehand. Maybe there was a Big Bang, but I believe something must have been there to start with. Whatever the subtleties which define God, and maybe God isn't a person living up in the spiritual realm, this God or Universal Consciousness must have created everything, somehow.

Cosmos seems to be a better word than *Universe*, as the definition of Cosmos, a Greek word, means both *order* and *world*, because the ancient Greeks thought that the world was perfectly harmonious and impeccably put in order. This is exactly in line with the conclusions David Gaggin comes to, which to me seem to explain everything in a much more satisfactory way. Apparently, there is no such thing as coincidence, the whole universe is meticulously planned and our life plan is detailed down to the last minuscule event. When something serendipitous happens, or something that seems to us like an incredible coincidence, actually it is what the spirits have planned and put into effect. It's just that we're not consciously aware of what this plan is, so when it happens, it just seems so extraordinary.

Again, the Western scientists' view of life, that it happened by some incredible accident and then life evolved into what we are today, doesn't make sense to me. There is so much information within a living person, or any creature, that, in my view, DNA cannot explain the majority of traits within a living thing. It is inconceivable to me that for instance, all the instincts of an animal, say, like a dog, could be stored within their DNA. Some dogs' behaviour is inherited from their parents and their parents before that and is completely different to another similar breed of dog from another family. I haven't yet heard scientists say that *this is the gene that creates this behaviour*. This is where Rupert Sheldrake's theory of *Morphic Fields* makes so much sense. When a creature develops as an embryo, it is being influenced by the Morphic Fields all around, and as the creature gets older and starts accumulating memories, these memories are shared, and all other creatures have access to them. This makes a lot more sense to me. I haven't heard neuroscientists say that *this is the part of the brain where all our memories are stored*. A computer has whole regions of memory where software and data are kept. For our DNA to be able to instruct our bodies to have all these various subtleties would surely require information of the order of several sets of Encyclopaedia Britannica, and massive as DNA is in terms of information encoded within its form, it seems to me the information stored within DNA is a tiny fraction of what would be needed to create the complexity which living creatures inherently have within themselves.

To me, the Western scientists' view is way too simplistic, and seems to exist in this too-simple form so that scientists don't have to provide any awkward explanations of why their knowledge is so sadly lacking, both to explain memory, and also to explain psychic abilities, which are a proven quality that living creatures have – already proven by totally valid and rigorous scientific tests carried out by scientists who don't subscribe to the predominantly blinkered view of the majority. There's pig-headedness, then there's irrational super-scepticism, an unwillingness to even consider the evidence of the *supernatural*. This seems to be the mindset of *conventional* scientists.

I've struggled most of my life since being a teenager with trying to understand what the point of life is. If, as I used to think until the last few years, there isn't an afterlife, which is what I thought, and is what Roger thought, then life is pretty pointless, isn't it? If we're all going to die, and that's the complete end of us, there hardly seems any point in dragging out that life until a natural death, which could well be an unpleasant downhill slide into ill-health and possibly also an unpleasant and uncomfortable death at the very end.

The incontrovertible proof that Joan and Roger have given us, that there is an afterlife, and the knowledge I found reading many books, that we reincarnate, and our spirit or soul has eternal life, has made my lifetime's quest for the answers all finally slot into place and now it all makes complete sense. Life has been planned meticulously, every detail thought of, and our physical death is merely us returning to our natural spiritual home, while we recuperate and contemplate our lessons from that physical life, before we decide to be reborn into a new physical life where we will learn some different lessons in our new physical adventure.

One quality that spirits possess, according to many experts, is that they can be in several or all places, at once. Joan and Roger on camera have not proved this beyond doubt, but when they have relayed their messages through a medium such as Liz Murphy in the US, whilst simultaneously showing as a spirit in our UK living room, this does pretty much suggest that they are in at least two places simultaneously. Even if this proof isn't conclusive, the concept really does seem to be the right one to explain so much. Maybe in the future, somehow, Roger will prove this beyond doubt, on camera, but until that day, I'm happy to accept it as the likeliest theory.

Knowing all of these subtleties and ins and outs of what life is, will make us live our physical lives differently. One of the biggest lessons of all within this concept of the afterlife is that people who take their own lives because they're having a difficult time here on Earth, and this particularly applies to younger men, are not doing themselves any favours – it just means they're going to have to come back again, to try and relearn their lessons here on Earth; suicide is not an easy way out, it's just going to create more problems in the future. If all the people who were considering suicide knew 100% that there is an afterlife then maybe they wouldn't choose this route but would try harder to resolve their difficult situation here on Earth.

Often at Stephen Holbrook shows he has brought through people who have committed suicide, and in probably every case I've heard they always regret doing what they did. Of course they leave behind distraught families, but also, they realise that they made a very big mistake and are sorry for what they did.

I suspect that if they had known that they would still be alive in the afterlife after losing their physical body, they would not have made the same choice.

So, finally, I need to thank Joan and Roger for opening my eyes to what life and death is all about. Roger's mission in his life on Earth was to teach people and educate them, and certainly in the afterlife he has carried on his teaching vocation by teaching me that the afterlife is real. This knowledge has made me research everything I can, through books and other means, to try and fully understand what the afterlife is. What I have found out so far is so utterly incredible, it really has been the biggest revelation of my life.

I hope you who have read this book will be as inspired as we have been, to investigate further, and to find out all you can about what is in store for all of us when we finish our physical life on this planet we currently inhabit. Won't it be lovely when we are all reunited with our loved ones? Isn't it so comforting to know that they really are still living in the afterlife, which is all around us, that their physical death didn't mean that they had actually died and stopped existing, but merely that they had lost their physical body and were still alive in the spirit world, still watching over us?

Good luck to all of you in your own individual quests, and please remember, if there's anything more I can help you with, I will be very happy to do whatever I can for you.

I would welcome any of your own thoughts, insights, or questions:

j.spillane@sky.com

Follow the latest news on Joan and Roger's story on social media:

Facebook: Alive in the Afterlife

YouTube: Joan and Roger Alive in the Afterlife on Camera

Instagram: Jeremy Spillane spirit greeter

Website: aliveintheafterlife.co.uk

Afterword

I had struggled to get the final fully formatted and edited manuscript ready to upload to Sixth Books by the agreed date. I delayed the due date by a month, so giving me time to wrap up all the various admin tasks before the book was committed to print.

With less than 48 hours to go, I was feeling happy that my project of the past two and a half years was on target to be delivered and could then go through the lengthy process of being transformed into a physical book, available to buy in real bookshops.

The whole project had gone surprisingly smoothly, all things considered, with just one major change of plan for the book last summer. I was happy with the front cover design – Roger had used ghost hunting equipment to show himself to us, so it was entirely appropriate that the front cover showed real photographic evidence from the SLS camera – one of the ghost hunting devices. Also, the wording on my front cover design was in line with advice I had read by successful authors, about what a front cover had to do, in order to appeal to potential readers.

I was more than happy that I had changed the title to include Joan, as initially the whole book was about what Roger had done – as Liz Murphy remarked when relaying Roger's and Joan's messages, "It's all about him." As Joan had started this whole afterlife revelation business, it was only fair her name was part of the book's title.

I was also more than happy that I was crediting Roger, posthumously, with being the co-author of the book. Roger had definitely instigated this whole project, and I wanted to acknowledge that. As books were Roger's passion, I owed it to him to not take all the credit, but to openly thank him for starting this whole story off, and for very literally planting his words in my mind. Most of the book just poured out of me, and I believe that could only be because he was actually writing the book, in a disembodied spiritual way.

The bits I thought would be hard – finding proof of Roger on the ghost hunting equipment – turned out to be easy. The difficult parts have been getting people to listen and to believe me. Maybe that's inevitable – proving life after death was possibly always going to be near impossible, no matter how good the evidence. Maybe humans don't want to believe this other-worldly explanation of life and death – perhaps our physical human brains can't handle the truth!

Does all the evidence on camera mean nothing – is it all just technology glitches and faults creating images that only look like something real to my overactive imagination?

How do we explain two SLS cameras both seeing a spirit at the same time?

Are both cameras faulty in exactly the same way?

What about the flying angel/birdlike thing which Caroline filmed on her iPhone, while looking out the window at work?

How can a camera create the illusion of an other-worldly entity, complete with beating wings, visible in great detail in the separated frames of the video?

I still believe Joan and Roger have genuinely made themselves known to us since they died. I accept that none of my so-called proof can be 100% convincing to everyone, but I truly hope that on the balance of probabilities, some of the readers of this book will be convinced. Joan's and Roger's proof is probably as good as it gets, and I am so grateful and in awe of them, for taking the trouble to show Caroline and me what they have.

If this is not really them, then I sincerely apologise for wasting everyone's time. Unless Joan and Roger are able to give us something better, then for now, I'm happy to believe it's them.

I hope some of you will agree.

References

Books

Gaggin, David, *Our Eternal Existence*, Washington, Sixth Books, 2023

Newton, Michael, *Journey of Souls*, St. Paul, Llewellyn, 1994

Pickering, John and Hall, Katie, *Beyond Photography*, Ropley, O Books, 2006

Sheldrake, Rupert:

The Presence of the Past/Morphic Resonance and the Habits of Nature, Icon Books, 2011

Dogs That Know When Their Owners Are Coming Home: And Other Unexplained Powers of Animals, Arrow, 2000

The Sense of Being Stared At: And Other Aspects of the Extended Mind, Arrow, 2004

TV Series

Paranormal Caught on Camera, Discovery Plus Channel, 7 series, 2019 on

Surviving Death, based on book by Leslie Kean, Netflix, 6 episodes, 2021

Film

The Secret, by Rhonda Byrne, TS Productions LLC, 2007

ALL THINGS PARANORMAL

Investigations, explanations and deliberations on the paranormal, supernatural, explainable or unexplainable. 6th Books seeks to give answers while nourishing the soul: whether making use of the scientific model or anecdotal and fun, but always beautifully written.

Titles cover everything within parapsychology: how to, lifestyles, alternative medicine, beliefs, myths and theories.

If you have enjoyed this book, why not tell other readers by posting a review on your preferred book site?

Recent Bestsellers from 6th Books Are:

The Scars of Eden
Paul Wallis
How do we distinguish between our ancestors' ideas of God and close encounters of an extraterrestrial kind?
Paperback: 978-1-78904-852-0 ebook: 978-1-78904-853-7

The Afterlife Unveiled
Stafford Betty
What the dead are telling us about their world!
What happens after we die? Spirits speaking through mediums know, and they want us to know.
This book unveils their world...
Paperback: 978-1-84694-496-3 ebook: 978-1-84694-926-5

Harvest: The True Story of Alien Abduction
G.L. Davies
G.L. Davies's most-terrifying investigation yet reveals one woman's terrifying ordeal of alien visitation, nightmarish visions and a prophecy of destruction on a scale never before seen in Pembrokeshire's peaceful history.
Paperback: 978-1-78904-385-3 ebook: 978-1-78904-386-0

M.E. Myself and I: Diary of a Psychic
Nicky Alan
A brutally honest journey showing strength of the human spirit, faith in the unseen and a tenacious will to survive.
Paperback: 978-1-78904-451-5 ebook: 978-1-78904-452-2

Phantoms of Christmas Past

Paul Weatherhead

True stories of seasonal ghost hoaxes and strange phantom panics from the nineteenth and early twentieth centuries.

Paperback: 978-1-80341-840-7 ebook: 978-1-80341-866-7

Spirit Release

Sue Allen

A guide to psychic attack, curses, witchcraft, spirit attachment, possession, soul retrieval, haunting, deliverance, exorcism and more, as taught at the College of Psychic Studies.

Paperback: 978-1-84694-033-0 ebook: 978-1-84694-651-6

Advanced Psychic Development

Becky Walsh

Learn how to practise as a professional, contemporary spiritual medium.

Paperback: 978-1-84694-062-0 ebook: 978-1-78099-941-8

Where After

Mariel Forde Clarke

A journey that will compel readers to view life after death in a completely different way.

Paperback: 978-1-78904-617-5 ebook: 978-1-78904-618-2

Paranormal Perspectives: One Big Box of 'Paranormal Tricks'?

John Fraser

Think Zen and the Art of Spending the Night in a Haunted House, a celebration of the dream of finding something undiscovered and different.

Paperback: 978-1-80341-524-6 ebook: 978-1-80341-532-1

Haunted: Horror of Haverfordwest

G.L. Davies

Blissful beginnings for a young couple turn into a nightmare after purchasing their dream home in Wales in 1989.

Paperback: 978-1-78535-843-2 ebook: 978-1-78535-844-9

Astral Projection Made Easy and overcoming the fear of death

Stephanie June Sorrell

From the popular Made Easy series, Astral Projection Made Easy helps to eliminate the fear of death through discussion of life beyond the physical body.

Paperback: 978-1-84694-611-0 ebook: 978-1-78099-225-9

Developing Your Supernatural Awareness

Fredrick Woodard

The common themes and details pointed out in this book will develop or enhance your understanding of our supernatural awareness and connection with our interactive universe.

Paperback: 978-1-80341-478-2 ebook: 978-1-80341-479-9

Readers of ebooks can buy or view any of these bestsellers by clicking on the live link in the title. Most titles are published in paperback and as an ebook. Paperbacks are available in traditional bookshops. Both print and ebook formats are available online.

Find more titles and sign up to our readers' newsletter at **www.6th-books.com**

Join the 6th books Facebook group at **6th Books The world of the Paranormal**